APPROACHES TO ENGLISH LANGUAGE TEACHING

Approaches To English Language Teaching

Dr. Joseph C. Mukalel
M.A., L.Ph., M.A. (U.K.), Ph.D.

DISCOVERY PUBLISHING HOUSE
NEW DELHI—110 002

Published by:

DISCOVERY PUBLISHING HOUSE PVT. LTD.
4383/4B, Ansari Road, Darya Ganj
New Delhi-110 002 (India)
Phone : +91-11-23279245; 23253475; 43596065
E-mail : discoverybooksindia@gmail.com
discoverypublishinghouse@gmail.com
namitwasan9@gmail.com
web : www.discoverypublishinggroup.com

***First Published:* 1998**

***Reprinted:* 2022**

ISBN: 978-81-7141-400-0

Approaches to English Language Teaching

Printed at:
Infinity Imaging Systems
Delhi

Introduction

English Language Teaching today has assumed dimensions that go for beyond the grip of an ordinary classroom teacher unless he is willing to apply his mind in a professional manner for enhancing the quality of his classroom teaching. This is true chiefly because an area like ELT has become a highly specialised on with components and implications well grounded on language teaching theories which can no longer be simply taken for granted by the teacher of English and thereby shut his eyes before such a reality as ELT theory and practices. ELT has become almost a discipline in itself and an expertise in this field of knowledge can now come only after years of painstaking training.

What does English language teaching man ? ELT is a field of theory and practices and a body of knowledge that consists of three major areas : 1. The structure of English language as such, 2. English Language Teaching Methodology, and 3. Materials Preparation for ELT. These three areas have become so highly specialised that there is plenty for an ELT expert to focus on any one and exclusively concentrate on it. With so much of information around a teacher of English today can no longer afford to brush aside an unnecessary this information which aims directly at him as the classroom practitioner and helps him teach most effectively. When ELT deals with 'the Structure of English Language' we embark first on what I prefer to call the foundations of ELT : 1. Theoretical Linguistics 2. Psycholinguistics and 3. Sociolinguistics. These three disciplines constitute the first and remote foundation of ELT a training in which makes a world of difference in the English teacher's perception of ELT and the work he is expected to do in the classroom.

The second foundation is most proximate to ELT and constitutes what we have called the *Approaches to English Language Teaching*. Against the background of the first and remote foundations, these approaches constitute, again, a body of knowledge which links in several ways the first foundations with actual classroom practices. Hence these approaches are the proximate body of knowledge which can guide the teacher as a classroom practitioner. It is this *theory structure* as we might call this body of knowledge, that should guide the teacher as to how to go about with the teaching of English in the classroom. Chapter 3 of the book takes care of what exactly the role of these approaches in ELT is.

The teacher of English is expected to have a basic understanding of what the *nature of language* is. This constitutes some rudiments of linguistics as to what the fundamental characteristics of language is. A purposeful and creative approach to language teaching indeed calls for some degree of insight into the nature of human language. The teacher is not a machine as occasionally we are made to believe. An effective utilisation of his creative resource will depend considerably on this understanding of the nature of human language in general and English language in particular. Language is no longer regarded as a body of abstractions to be talked about in the classroom. Language is more today a communicative event and only its purposeful and creative use in the classroom can solve most problems related to the learning of English in India as a second language.

Teaching a second language like English in the classroom is thought of as a simulation of the first language learning strategies of the L_1 learner in the family. An understanding of the *Acquisition of the First language* is therefore an important component of the teacher's battery of information while deciding his own classroom strategies for teaching English. The forbearance that is required of a teacher and the role of classroom interaction for giving shape to adequate *English language atmosphere* are far too significant for the teacher to neglect. It is in this atmosphere that adequate *internalization* should take place. The teacher functions only as the agent and custodian of this language atmosphere.

An approach to English language teaching that has been almost universal, most traditional and historically evolved has come to be called *Grammar-Translation Method.* This is the unique method which automatically teachers fall back on to when they are not guided by more enlightened, modern and effective approaches to ELT. Grammar-translation method is still used in the teaching of classical languages. The present work attempts to acquaint the teacher with the nature of this panacea that make him aware of the major drawbacks of this method in teaching English.

The history of English language teaching in India is a history of *structural approach.* With the introduction of structural approach ended on era of English language teaching which was marked by a speculative, meaning-oriented, and formal grammar based teaching of English. Formal grammar teaching and translation was lifted out of the classroom. Structural approach laid emphasis on the teaching of English through a systematic teaching of the *grammatical structures* of the language. The most outstanding characteristic of structural approach is the graded presentation of these structures with textbooks and instructional materials prepared on its basis.

The major drawback in the application of structural approach was its link with direct method. The initial English language teaching strategy promulgated by the Government of India was the structural approach guided by the principles of direct method. It is after the 60's that structural approach in our country came to be de-linked from direct method and our English language teaching strategy came to be called *New Structural Approach.*

Direct method came in the West as a sharp reaction to the grammar-translation method. In grammar-translation method we find an extreme and exclusive emphasis on formal grammar, reading and writing as well as translation from and into the mother-tongue as a regular classroom technique. Direct method on the other hand advocated the teaching of the foreign language *without* the medium of the mother-tongue, a total avoidance of the pupil's mother-tongue in the classroom, and exclusive focus on the listening-speaking skill of the language. Direct method, a product of the second World War came to be modified for a variety of reasons and there came a modified version of it in the garb of the *audio-lingual* approach. Audio-lingual approach is a highly linguistics-biased approach to the teaching of English. The stress of structuralist linguists on the speech form of language and their belief that the spoken language is the real language are reflected in the audio-lingual approach. Since a much greater quantum of theory is at its disposal to support it, this trend has come to be labelled an approach to foreign language teaching.

Extreme viewpoints have always given birth to new trends in English language teaching. Bilingual method is one such trend in the teaching of English as a foreign or second language. This trend sprang up in reaction to both the practices of direct method and audio-lingual approach. Both these trends advocated the total neglected of the learner's mother-tongue in the English class-room. Such an extremist strategy left a section of ELT experts unconvinced of the effect of these approaches that gave no place of the mother-tongue in the learning of English in the classroom. It was thought that the *legitimate and well-defined* use of the learner's mother-tongue can be of great help in the teaching of English and such a practice can get rid of a whole lot beating round the bush in making the learner understand the meaning and use of new language items. This trend has come to be known as bilingual method. It tries to restore the learner's mother-tongue its legitimate place in the teaching of a foreign or second language.

It has always been the view that teaching English should be done in such a way that the English classroom provides adequate atmosphere for learning English as the medium of communicative functions. But most recently this perspective of ELT began attracting considerable attention in ELT circles and has given birth to what has come to be called *Communicative Language Teaching*. Communicative language teaching puts premium on the use of English as communicate acts, and for communicative functions. Teaching becomes task-oriented. The classroom becomes an arena for role-plays and activities simulating the actual communicative situation in which the native speaker uses the language. The syllabus itself is designed not on grammatical structures but on communicative functions for which structures are employed.

Teaching English in India has become a complex affair and the problems that arises in our approach to ELT are multidimensional. No one approach to ELT can be our panacea as each of these ELT dimensions call for different solutions. We have universities that are of purely English medium and other universities where English is just a compulsory subject. Between these two extremes we have a wide variety of situations for which suitable ELT methodology needs to be developed. Our post-graduate students should be saved from the kind of disillusionment they are experiencing at present from their lack of proficiency in English. The chapter on *Teaching English in Universities* deal with these problems and recommends feasible solutions.

English medium schools in our country are looked upon by our politicians as a menace to our national development. That is only a platform jargon. English medium schools are our most potential resource in this country so far as ELT is concerned. But this resource is again left untapped for a variety of reasons. It is often presumed that teaching English in English medium schools is beyond all methods and can be a hodge-podge affair. Hence the poor state of affairs in this sector. The chapter on *Teaching English in English medium schools*. Discusses these problems and recommends a viable methodology for teaching English.

It is high time that we take the problem of teaching English in our country more seriously and save it from political morass. Political considerations should not be permitted to bias our attitudes and alter the right directions we are committed to. The teacher of English needs to develop not only the right perspective but make attempts to tap the resources of right language teaching methodology that should be one of his fundamental commitments. This he should approach in a systemic and scientific manner so that he is in a position to imbibe the latest trends in English language teaching. To do this the teacher of English requires the foundations on which to build the information with which he is fed further as a classroom practitioner. Elt has become an established discipline in our country and it is high time that the teacher of English in India stops groping in the dark in order to undertake effective classroom teaching, and utilize the resources put at his disposal for the purpose.

Contents

1

The Nature of Language

1. Language as a Structured System

Man confronts all kinds of reality around him, and the puzzling questions that hang over him like the impending sword of Damocles are the 'why? and what' ? of things. The myriad of stars above him has become the object of his observation just as his own physical body, the many in one, a *unity* in a sort of *multiplicity*. Down the ages man has discovered that stars in their infinitude are not so scattered and orderless as they seem to be, and the human body, though apparently one, consists of microsegments of material units. The order and super-organisation found in the stellar and the solar realms we call a *system*; and the unity of many in the one human body we call a *structure*.

But there is phenomenon that has aroused in us more curiosity and interest than any other own the ages: Language. Language is concrete and abstract; language is one and many: and it reveals all the characteristics of both a structure and a system. A close observation of a set of utterances produced by man reveals the fact that it is not an unanalysable, indivisible thing. An *utterance*, a spoken sentence or what may be called a unit of discourse, *e.g. The boy is ill*, affects the auditory organs of the listener in terms of certain units of *sounds. e.g.* /b/, /ɔi/, /i/. This most extrinsic layer or component of language is called the *phonological component*. A systematic study of the structure of this component is the *phonology* of the Language. Going further deep into the language in terms of the utterances under consideration, the linguistics-scientist discovers that the sound set of units which are themselves further analyzable, are combined into patterns of sequences based on some specifications of meanings which the sequences of sounds are intended to reveal. The linguist calls these minimum meaningful units morphemes *e.g.* boy, -s, fall, -ing. The branch of linguistics which takes care of these meaningful components and their structure in the language is *Morphology*.

The structural organization of the language does not end with that. On observing the sentences of the language we find that the *words* and the *morphemes* are ordered in a definite manner, and that each utterance has a structure to reveal exactly as each word of the language has a definite *structure*. This ordering of the words into phrases, phrases into clauses and further into sentences is the *syntactic component* of the language. e.g. *The boy is ill* by contrast to *Is the boy ill* ?. A study of this component forms the *syntax* part of *linguistics*.

The entire range of language is not susceptible to the senses. The auditory organs are able to sense or receive only the most extrinsic components of language. As we have examined to some extent there is the much more to language than this extrinsic aspect. Ferdinand De Saussure, the initiator of modern linguistics speaks of the *expression* and the *content* aspects of language. That language also consists of something not susceptible to the pure senses is a fact known from time immemorial. This aspect of language which in fact makes up it core is the *semantic component* of the language. The specialised area in linguistics which studies this semantic component is semantics. In the sentence *'Ill is boy the'* though the syntax is damaged, it makes sense to a native speaker because of its semantic integrity. The structure of language consists of all the above mentioned components. Each has a definite place in the system *i.e. language*. One is not the other, although the demarcations are not easy to define. Language is a *structured* system: one composed of several elements organized with a view to functioning for a definite purpose. This chief purpose of language is communication. All the elements are organized to achieve this target.

2. Language is for Communication

Eventhough the role of language for purposes of communication was always emphasized, present-day linguistics has become all the more aware of this *teleological* role of language. Although modern linguistics studies all aspects of language and all kinds of language including the language of literature, the most adequate data for purposes of linguistic investigation and description are the spoken utterances of language used for the purpose of communication among the individuals of a given linguistic community.

It happens that a man comes home all wet from the rain outside, and his wife after having seen the heavy rain outside and the way the man has come home asks him, *Oh ! You are all wet' aren't you?.* Linguistically speaking, this is no question at all. She expects no answer in the true sense of the term. The facts that is was raining and that the man was wet all over were obvious enough to the speaker and the listener. The environment of the particular utterance did not call for any *information* to be conveyed, or as what we may say, any *intention* to be fulfilled. The utterance did not achieve either an informational or an international target. It was just a way of speaking and reacting to a given situation, without expecting an informative answer. As we shall examine later in the section on communication, no communication in the proper sense of the term took place in the above context.

Communicability is the essence of human language. Any utterance, any discourse, as we may call it, takes place in a context where at least two individuals must be present. The teleological nature of language is not present in a context where some one is merely soliloquizing. Soliloqui is sheer thinking aloud. All of us have experiences of having heard someone or other speaking to himself at some situations, especially of excessive joy or sorrow. Communication proper is teleological. It begins from an individual and terminates in another. Linguistics concerns itself not with soliloquies primarily but language as employed for purposes of communication in socio-cultural contexts.

3. Language is Symbolic

If communication takes place between human individuals,

how exactly does language pass from one to another? An answer to this calls for technical support from biology, acoustic physics and communication engineering. But linguistics tackles this problem to a certain extent. Language Functions in terms of *signs* and *symbols*. A sign is a representative mode, it represents a unit of meaning. From the commonsense viewpoint a sign stand for something else. A sign doesn't function on its own right. It is always *representative*. A symbol is a much more complex notion than a sign. A sign conveys a unit of meaning; a symbol, in the true sense of the term, represents a complex reality, or a set of values.

Both these notions are equally applicable to the reality of language at various levels. Language has sign functions and symbolic functions. In other words language has sign values and symbolic values. The speaker, a physical entity has no way of penetrating the mind of the listener who is another physical entity, except through a medium that makes such a thing possible. The expression features of the language which themselves are set of physical entities (because they are susceptible to the sense of audition) function as bearers of the content features of language. This is how it becomes physically possible for man to communicate. The language elements produced by the articulatory organs of the speaker are conveyed through a medium (*e.g.* air) in terms of the acoustic principles, and received by the auditory organs of the listener in their audio-modality. The listener receives the element of information contained in the content specifications of the language.

In otherwords what the articulatory organs produce and the organs of audition receive are "meaning carriers" or words and utterances that function as a symbol. The symbolic value, at the extrinsic level, is thus attached to the words and their combinations is meaningful order. At one level this is what we understand by language functioning as *symbolic*. There is another aspect to the same at a still deeper level. The relation that exists in a linguistic context in terms of the elements involved may be represented schematically as follows:

	3	Verbal symbols	1
		↑ ↓	
Language	2	Conceptual elements	2
		↑ ↓	
	1	Features of experience	3

There are three layers that require consideration. We have seen that the verbal features (elements of the utterance) function as symbolic bearers of the specifications of meanings or the concepts. But are concepts or meanings end in themselves? This is where the second and deeper functions of symbolism come in. The meaning specifications, as we may call them, represent deeper levels of reality or what we may call the actual experience of individuals. Therefore human language functions at a two-level representation: at the level of concepts and at the level of experience or reality.

It is the symbolic features of language, in fact, that make it an effective medium for communication as well as for all characteristic uses for which human language is employed. Language is structured in such a way that several physical and metaphysical elements go into the making of it. This *unity* makes language all that it is.

4. The Vocal Characteristic of Language

There are over three thousand languages in the world. This overwhelming number of human languages are all attached to a particular community which we may call a linguistic community. All these languages have had their natural growth along with the progress and formation of the community. In otherwords we seldom, if ever, find a language which is not used in the speech-habits of a community. All natural languages (opposed to those that have been constructed by linguists) have had their origin in speech. It all began with some community trying to communicate among the individuals. The initial growth and development of any such language sprang up from the individuals who communicated for purposes of social interaction.

In otherwords, language, above all, is *speech*. The written forms are all mere frozen representations of what the individual speakes, or supposed to be speaking. Not that there is less nobility in reading or in writing, but that speech takes predominance over wrighting so far as language priorities are concerned. Language is thus, vocal. This vocal language forms the 'primary data' of linguistics. In this context we may say that language is the product of the vocal or articulatory faculties of man. Language is characterized by these vocal features of man. It is very much restricted and determined by these vocal features. However intelligent a man may be, he will be handicapped so far as the spoken language is concerned if his vocal organs do not function properly.

There are several reasons for us to believe that language is basically speech. Some of the chief reasons are the following: (1) The origin of all natural languages is in speech; (2) Communication in a linguistic community can be had only through speech; (3) speaking and listening are skills which naturally develop; (4) speech requires no other external tools to function; (5) speech achieves the quickest communication; (6) the individual's specifications and characteristics reflect much more in speech than in writing; (7) speech habits reflect the changes in a language more than writing does; (8) speech is as though living and evolving; it is the most dynamic element of society.

For all these reasons modern linguistics has been emphasizing the spoken form of language. As we shall examine later, the reasons mentioned above have made speech the centre of attention in all modern foreign language teaching methods. Today speech is considered the primary form of language and speech forms the primary data for linguistic research. But some of the latest approaches to language have attempted to revive the emphasis on the written form of language on an equal footing.

5. The Arbitrariness of Language

In several senses language is *arbitrary*. It is a property of human language that has several deeper implications than it would seem to us. Take for instance the word '*man*'. To the native English speaker or to any one very much conversant with the English language the word '*man*' is something taken for granted. One seldom asks the question if the word means anything. But at the same time, to a foreign language speaker who is not conversant with English, '*man*' is a non-sense unit. It may even sound ridiculous to a native speaker of another language, because a similar word may mean something quite funny.

What happens here? What makes the word '*man*' an absolute stranger to a non-English speaker? It can be explained only through the arbitrariness of language. The following illustration is helpful in understanding this property of language.

(The symbolic representation for '*human being*' in the specific sense)

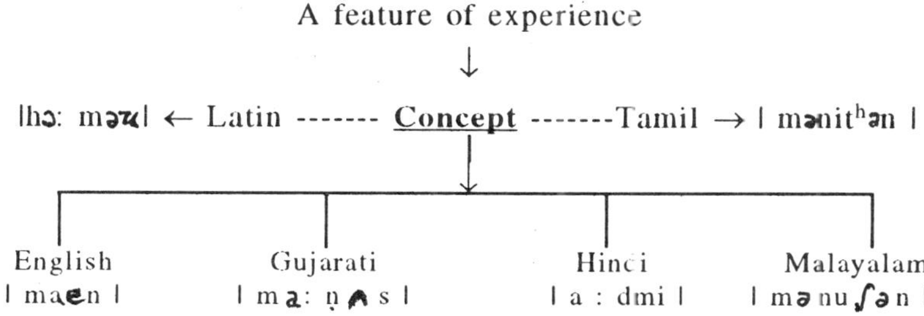

The meaning element '*man*' (in the specific sense of the term) is expressed in very different ways in different languages. The meaning element here is a fact of human experience, and therefore forms a part of any language man speaks. But on examining various languages we find that each language has some distinct unit of language to express this concept. It means that there exists no one to one correspondence, or any basic, essential corresponding between the *form* chosen to express the sense, and the *sense* or signification itself. This is the essence of linguistic arbitrariness.

There are several other levels of arbitrariness in language. There is practically no rationale behind the way the sound clusters, the word forms, the phrases or the idioms are structured. All this developed due to the force of convention which played most significant role in language development. Again, the usage, the structural forms, the sentence patterns are all proofs of the arbitrary nature of language. Almost the entire component of the *expression* part of language developed arbitrarily. But each of these aspects became a norm in language once the usage was accepted by the majority of those who had the last say in the affairs of the community. This property of the language shows that no part of the *expression* aspect of language can be an absolutely permanent feature.

6. Language is Changing

Changeability as a major property of language came to be

emphasized only in modern linguistics. This goes very much against the notions held by the philosophical grammars of the Middle and early Modern Ages. The changeability of language was not a characteristic feature in the context of 'Universal Grammar'. 'Universal Grammar' held the belief that the grammars of all language in the world were the same and consequently the structure of Greek or Latin could be a basis for describing any language. In other words more or less language was looked upon as a phenomenon of unchanging characteristics, and the changing aspects such as those features of the spoken language were not considered significant.

But with the onset of Modern Linguistics, especially structuralism, emphasis was placed on the spoken form of language. With this some new insights into the structure of language came to develop. Language is no longer studied as an unchanging, wholly absolute phenomenon. Today stress is put on the changing characteristics as well. As the spoken form of language came to be emphasized, and insights are developed with regards to the changing nature of the spoken language, the role of *change* in language came to receive considerable attention.

In fact almost all aspects of language in one way or other undergo change. Although extreme, it could be said that language is in a state of flux, meaning that *change* pervades every component of language. Examining the *phonology* of language, one finds that it undergoes change in long periods of time.

The set of sounds, the vowels, the consonants, the diphthongs, the triphthongs and the sound clusters of Old English period were not very much the same used in the middle English. *Cu: monne, sunne* and *childe* etc. are not understood today. In otherwords there is a large scale give and take in the phonology of the language, as languages have come into more and more intimate contact.

The *morphology* of the language changes from time to time. The Old English was a highly inflécted language; the inflectional suffixes *i.e.* chiefly the declensions and conjugation were reduced to the minimum in the Middle English. As English language developed in tune with the requirements of the times, the present day English retains exceptionally few inflectional endings. All that today English language has one the following : (1) the plural suffix $\{-Z_1\}$ (2) The genitive suffix $\{-Z_2\}$, the third singular suffix $\{-Z_3\}$, the past time suffix $\{-D_1\}$ the past participle suffix $\{-D_2\}$ and the gerund as well as present participle suffix {–iŋ}. Added to these we have the adjective suffixes {–∂r} and {–∂st}. This shows a constant change in the forms of language.

The *syntax* of language is another component that affects change. There are several very basic structural aspects that remain more or less the same throughout, such as the basic ordering of a sentence. We do not know of any period in English when the subject as a rule was placed at the end of a sentence. But the surface ordering of the language, the structuring of phrases, the use of the pronouns, prepositions, articles, and the way the auxiliaries are employed have undergone changes from time to time. Similarly the *semantic structure* of language keeps on changing along with communal, social and cultural changes that affect the speech community. New experiences and new meanings supplement and substitute old ones.

There are several forces that affect change in languages. Owing to several circumstances languages come into mutual contact. Wars, travels, business and commercial relations between communities, new inventions and discoveries, social revolutions migration and a number of other factors play powerful roles in bringing languages together as well as in having new additions to the language. No language at any phase reveals any observable change. What we experience is only the cumulative affect of a continual change. A decade or two can hardly reveal any observable change in a language.

7. Language is Culture-based

The fact that any language is culture-based hardly needs any comment. It may require a full Volume to show the relation between language and culture. In the broadest sense *culture* is all that a people are: their ways of doing, thinking and believing as well as all the characteristics and things they possess. In the narrowest sense culture stands for the products of a society as society: the habits, beliefs and things handed down from generation to generation. Language in any sense of the term is a major component as well as the most complex element of culture. The language of a community contains the verbal replica of all aspects of its culture. At the same time language is a part of the culture of a community. Culture includes all aspects of the community's behaviour; language is socio-individual behaviour in the fullest sense of the term. Verbal behaviour *i.e.* language, is representative of all aspirations and beliefs of the society as well as it perpetuates those elements in a striking manner. One could not imagine a society without the ability to maintain communication among the individuals. Language is the embodiment of culture so far as all cultural elements somehow or other get embedded as a part of the verbal behaviour.

8. The Creative Nature of Language

One of the properties of language that has come to be emphasized only during the late twentieth century is the creative aspect of language. Noam Chomsky's writings have placed the creative aspect of language in the right perspective. Language functions in a stimulous-reinforcement—response context, all right. But this is not the whole of language. Nothing else but *linguistic creativity* can explain the fact that a human child with his relative mastery of a language is in a position to produce sentences that are fully original, sentences that perhaps no one has ever uttered before or those that the child has never heard any one uttering before. This unique capacity to organise and produce new sentences of a language is called linguistic creativity. B.F. Skinner's dictum of language being purely a *stimulus-response* product is counteracted in Chomsky's notion of linguistic creativity. This is very relevant to our context here because this concept provides several new insights into the language teaching-learning process. Language in the classroom should be taught keeping in mind the creative potential of the child. The child is not a machine, nor is it like any other infra-human organism. The human child is a person with a lot of creative potency and intelligence functioning in a social set up.

9. The Uniqueness of Language

Languages are unique in themselves. Based on this principle

Modern Linguistics has ventured out to investigate into the structures of language. The belief was held earlier, as we saw in the section on the changeability of language, that the structures of all languages boil down to one and the same thing in the last analysis. Against this belief came the view that there is some level of specificity with regards to the components of each and every language, that no two things are exactly the same with two languages. The *phonology* of language is unique as different languages share in the 'total human sound resource' in different manner. No two languages have exactly the same set of consonants, vowels and their clusters. Similarly, the *morphological* aspects, the suffixes, the prefixes, the inflections and the component-formations differ from language to language. On the level of *syntax* too, languages are very different. Different languages have different structural ordering the rules of patterning words in sentences. Lastly and perhaps most important of all languages are different at the level of meanings. The foregoing discussion on the cultural implications of language helps us to understand how far the meaning component of languages differ among one another. No two languages are the same from all viewpoints.

10. A Few Other Characteristics

There are several other predominant features which languages reveal. One may examine a few important ones among those. It is some times said that only man is capable of telling a lie, that animals are not. It is true so far as language is concerned. Language is a means for man to express himself, but it is interesting to see that the same language helps him to hide things. It is a dual property of language, along with other dual properties as expression and content. For the famous philosopher Wittgenstein, the main function of language was to obscure and hide things. Perhaps he was right in the sense that language as expression has no one to one correspondence with meaning or content. All natural languages are so full of homophonous, homonymous, synonymous and ambiguous expressions that we do not always understand the language of others the way we think we do. This is where what we call 'misunderstanding' and 'misinter-pretations' arise. Languages have their natural metaphoric way of putting things. Also there are several levels and layers at which languages function.

The poet's language is not the philosopher's language, the mystic's language is different from the politician's language. Language places before the human mind problems that are puzzling and the interesting the thing is that all these problems regarding language can be dealt with using only the same human language.

2
Acquicision of the First Language

1. Learning Conditions of L_1 and L_2

There is a world of difference between the child learning or rather acquiring his native language and the adult acquiring a foreign language. In our understanding of the *acquisition process* of a language these two situations may be considered types : the learning of L_1 *i.e.* one or more languages learned in the family environment, in absolutely congenial circumstances without the cumbersome activities of the classroom. In India especially it is a usual phenomenon that a child is required to learn more than one language as its first languages without any one conspicuously predominating the others. There are several possible variations among what we may call : the *mother tongue i.e.* the language of the parents (it also happens that the parents belong to different linguistic communities), the local language, the regional language, and the national language. It happens that a child from the very beginning comes in touch with and is compelled to learn quite a few of these variety of languages. It is not possible for us to differentiate the learning processes of those languages as each of these has similar or the same *learning environment*. Therefore in the present work by L_1 we mean all the languages mentioned above *i.e.* the set of languages that a child picks up before the school-going age.

By L_2 we do not mean the 'second language' which the child picks up, the second language for an Indian boy may be Hindi as the family comes to stay in a Hindi speaking region when the boy is three or four year old. By L_2 in the present work is meant what Robert Lado calls, 'the target language' or the languages the child learns at School. It may be another regional language of the country or it may be a foreign language. In this category for which we have an entirely different learning environment *i.e.* the classroom, we include a language like Hindi and a foreign language like English. Both these are learned in the classroom at the level of L_2. The distinction between L_1 and L_2 brought out here will be constantly referred to in the following pages. It should cause no misunderstanding in the minds of the readers when English language is referred to as L_2 in India.

The learning conditions of L_1 and L_2, against the background discussed above, differ vastly. The learning processes at these two levels are affected and influenced by several, factors and the very *process* of *acquisition* differs to a great extent. The L_1 is picked up at home, in the most natural situations, guided and controlled by those who are near and dear to the child. The L_2, on the other hand is learned in the most artificial situations, the overcrowded classroom, in an atmosphere of fear, anxiety and tension. The learning of the L_1 takesplace along with other aspects of biological growth such as walking; as it is said, the child walks and talks. Language learning is an integral part of the biological growth, it is paced and controlled by forces that do not create much of tension in the child as those in the classroom. The L_2 learning takesplace when the child's attention is scattered and pulled apart by several unrelated forces such as peergroup friendships and rivalries.

More than anything else the learning of the L_2 takesplace when the L_1 language or languages have already have already taken roots. The most refined and rudimentary language habits have been fashioned on the 'tabula rasa' of the child's linguistic potencies : both physiological and mental. The L_2 is introduced into such an actualized setting when the child's receptive potency has been considerably determined. Over and above these limitations, the classroom has a single teacher for several dozens of pupils while at home the single child is aided by several 'teachers' in the learning of the L_1. A very significant aspect in the learning of the L_1 which has conspicuous reference to the teaching of the L_2 is the natural adherence to the basic *principles* of *learning* as such. The child picks up linguistic elements which are easier and more useful to practical life earlier than what is more difficult and less useful. Similarly the child picks up the words for things and actions that are closer in his *experience*. Much before he learns words like *road*, *man* or *virtue*, the child comes to know words such as *water*, *milk*, *bed* and *food*. In other words the learning of the L_1 is governed by the principles of proximity, usefulness, concreteness, particularity and interest. In today's endeavour to teach foreign languages, in spite of all efforts and good will, this is one aspect where we have most miserably failed: seldom do present-day text books and teaching materials contain things which are most useful, concrete and interesting to the children of a given level.

The characteristic difference between the learning conditions of the L_1 and L_2 from the essential background for the teaching of L_2 in class. *Psycholinguistics* investigates into the integral aspects of the L_1 learning process, consequently trying to achieve two things : knowledge of the nature of language learning process as well as insights into the teaching of L_2.

2. Factors Affecting the Learning of L_1

An analysis of the conditions under which L_1 is picked up would reveal a variety of factors that effect the native language learning process.

(1) the *physical environment* influences the L_1 learning process. The material surroundings of a child have a lot to do with what and how he picks up a language. Much more than an adult the child gets truly involved in his material surroundings. The dog, the cat, the house, and the trees around the house have a lot to do with the way the child learns his first language.

(2) the *social environment* affects L_1 learning greatly. The child growing up with the parents, and an orphan child make a world of difference in language learning. The child whose mother goes out daily to work and the one who is always

by the mother's side pick up L_1 quite differently, however may the former make up for her absence. The mother, the family and the neighbourhood are social elements so essential to the natural language growth of the child. Sociological factors are more determining than anything else in the L_1 learning process.

(3) *Physical* and *economic resources* affect L_1 learning process. The language development of a child from an economically backward family has all the reasons to be hamphered in contrast to a child from a well-to-do family. Economic resources influence the child's contact with things and events and possibly limit the range of the child's overall experience. Economic factors determine to a great extent the feasibility of the parents to care for the language development of the child.

(4) The learning of L_1 has the most powerful *motivations* behind it. This is a unique characteristic of the first language or languages. There are compelling needs which are both *internal* as well as *external*.

(a) There are several internal needs which compel the child to learn his first language as quickly and perfectly as he can. Among these internal needs the most compelling ones are the need for food, warmth and shelter. These are of physiological nature. There are also emotional needs to fulfil such as the needs for constant care, love and affection. These needs cannot at all be met unless the child masters some kind of liaison devices with the world outside. The *first language* is the most essential of such devices.

(b) There are several needs and motivations which are external by nature. Social interaction, on the one hand for purposes mentioned above, and on the other for the fulfillment of the social urges of the child, requires mastery over a language for interaction with the members of society. There is the need for *self-expression* and *creative behaviour* which raises the human being far above the level of a sheer biological organism and requires the mastery of some languages as the medium of communication. The child not only makes use of the first language for functional purposes, but also more than anything else creatively enjoys himself by talking to the 'catty' and 'doggy'. This is an element that cannot be overlooked.

An outstanding feature of the early language learning experience is *egocentricity*. The child is highly egocentric; this egocentric attitude is reflected above all in the child's language learning experience. He picks up only the language items that are absolutely essential to expressing himself. He is the centre of his entire language experience. The first language is the chief means to get things done for himself, to assert himself to the social environment and to exert maximum control over his environment. The child feels that the whole world revolves around him. The pronouns he picks up at the outset are highly reflective of this egocentric nature : *I, me it, my, mine* are said to be the earliest pronouns the child picks up, it takes time before he begins using pronouns such as *we, us, our* etc. In short, language learning of the early period as well as the entire language learning experience is parallel to the development of the child's personality : it is a movement from 'the dim image of the mother' to an all pervading 'vision of humanity' as such.

3. Stages of L_1 Acquisition Process

Even though accounts by psycholinguistics on the first language acquisition process vary greatly and there has been no absolute agreement with regards to the phases of language development in children all over the world, there has been no doubt that the language development of children is fully *phased*. It takes place in terms of various definable stages which children in any part of the world are said to undergo although the chronological correspondence may not be the same. Attempts have been made to describe the learning of language by children in terms of *operant* and *classical conditioning*. Skinner expresses the view that these early operant responses take the form of 'mands', 'tacts' or 'echoic responses'. A mand is a demand in one word like 'milk', a tact is a naming response in which the child names some aspect of his environment and is variedly *rewarded* especially by the happiness of the mother. An *echoic* response is simply a repetition of his own or an adult's utterance, the reward being self-stimulation. These responses are further corrected, shaped and modified by the mother and other members of the family and the child learns to approximate adult utterances. *Rewarding* of the correct responses help consolidate these and progress towards accurate *verbal responses.*

As it is often described, the speech mechanism is a crude possibility. The child is at the birth endowed with the basic potencies for language in the form of the biological organs of speech as well as the inner faculties of speech co-ordination and production. These biological and mental faculties function as the substratum of language development.

The child living in an interacting with society, is continuously bombarded with the language of the society. But the earliest phases of language development do not seem to be much affected by what goes on around. The *first cry* of the infant functions as the crude starting point which makes possible all activities of the lungs and the speech organs. The earliest significant utterances of the infant are the *babbling sounds* characterized by a two-way system : the 'ba....ba, ma.....ma, pa....pa' sounds produced by the infant are conveyed to the brain centres as auditory impulses which further enable the infant to produce the same sounds again. It is described as a *vocal-ear reflex*, a self-stimulating and self-reinforcing phenomenon. Society is too dim to influence articulatory functions at this phase. We may describe this as the stage of random articulation.

The mother, representing society, is the motivating force behind the next phase, usually called by psycholinguistics as *echolalia*. The same or similar articulate elements are produced by the infant as the mother. Here the ego for the first time confronts the mother *i.e.* society. The mother utters the word 'doll' and the infant takes pleasure in repeating the possible echo *da*. There is a double—pronged *auditory excitement* that is caused by the mother as well as by the infant. *Echolalia* is thus described as an *ear-vocal reflex* : beginning with the mother's utterance and ending with the utterance by the infant. This is essentially a stage of very crude imitation, an exact imitation of the utterance by the adult being impossible for the infant. The organ for audition, the ear, plays a greater role at this phase of language develcpment.

In the stage following we find a *conditioning* of the *articulate elements* by objects and situations. This phase is characterized by the child's naming things as they are held out to or found by the child. It is described as the stage of an intense 'naming explosion'. A conditional responses is effected by the visual stimulation, to doll, with the verbal stimulus, the word doll. The sight of the doll along with the word doll enables the child to associate both and learn the word doll and remember it in connection with the thing, the doll.

In the following phase of the language learning process, the sight of the doll alone is enough for the child to evoke the world doll, the parent providing a visual stimulus to which the child is in a position to evoke a truly *verbal response*. The last stage in this process is linguistically very characteristic. Here a verbal stimulus alone can evoke a verbal response. Here the child has reached the realm of actual language. He is in a position to function at the level of symbolic language. The child can answer a question; the word doll can be used in answer to a question without any visual aid. The child begins to comprehend word symbols, not merely imitate sound units. He begins manipulating language items to his own advantage. Now, he is on the way to becoming what we call 'a linguistic adult' : capable of manipulating his language to meet all practical situations within the purview of the experiences of his own linguistic community. All that now remains is the intricate, idiomatic, abstract, artistic and professional language which he begins acquiring in society as a school-going child or otherwise.

4. Internalisation of Linguistic Systems

The entire language learning is a process of internalisation of systems. This has been clearly and systematically re-emphasized by Noam Chomsky in his works in transformational generative linguistics. This goes diametrically opposed to the stimulus-responses theories where attempt is made to explain all aspects of language process in terms of stimulus-response-reinforcement bond. Chomsky condemns the connectionism of skinner, which adheres to an explanation of all language phenomenon by means of behaviourist principles.

Section 3 of the present chapter deals with the sequential stages of the development of a child's language, but from a *psychological perspective*. Looking at language development from a purely *linguistic perspective*, it is wholly a process of internalisation : the functional aspects of language acquisition require more of a psychological description in terms of the patterns of behaviour; the structural aspects of language acquisition, on the other hand require a linguistic description in terms of the internalisation of linguistic systems. *Internalisation* of linguistic systems occur at a variety of levels. The infant at the early period of linguistic development lives in a language atmosphere. He is bombarded, so to say, by the language utterances of the people around, directed at him as well as otherwise. The earliest utterances of the child (see Sec. 3) known as *random articulation* are not in fact the exact feedback of this linguistic atmosphere constantly affecting the auditory organs of the child. This random articulation, by nature a *vocal-ear reflex*, is some kind of internal process stimulated by the pleasurable experiences of the child, the main stimulus being the *reflex* itself. It is a self stimulated activity as random articulation gathers momentum.

But once the infant's auditory organ begins reacting to the environment, the infant takes in whatever it can. At first the random articulation consists of non-distinctive sounds like those of the infra-human animals. These cannot be considered linguistic units, rather we call the random articulation sounds pre-linguistic, but forming the very foundation of later linguistic behaviour. The first system which the child takes in or rather *internalises* is the basic sound system of the language : the phonological system (see Section 5 of the present chapter). The elders speak in natural ways carrying on the affair of day to day life. It is not a teaching process. The 'teachers' live; the 'pupil' learns : both happen in an automatic, involuntary fashion. At this stage from all the language material the child listens to, the only thing that he internalises is the set of sounds. He, in otherwords, begins the process of producing the distinctive sounds which are basic to the language he begins to pick up.

While picking up the sound units the child is getting familiar with the basic *morphological sets* of the language, yet not in a position to produce them. The internalisation of the morphological units and full words takes place because much before production there is the comprehension of these items. The child follows the language of the elders eventhough he cannot actively communicate. With further development comes the period when the child not only follows but produces *words* not merely imitating the elders, but after having thoroughly internalized the *relation between the word and the feature of experience* which the word represents. Meanwhile, again, the language, full fledged and natural utterances of the elders go on. So far the child has been able to pick up the distinctive sounds and then the sequences of these sounds, the words from the language store of the elders. Before mastering the words, the *distinctive sounds* are combined into some sort of non-sense units which we often hear children speak. After the words internalised are in active use, these are employed in 'non-grammatical' utterances: incomplete and mixed up sentences. It takes time before any further development takes place, when the child is able to produce grammatical sentences. The internalisation of the basic grammar *i.e.* structural rules of the language, has been taking place as a result of the child's continuous acquaintance with adult language.

The process of internalisation takes place not only at the linguistic levels mentioned above, but also at the level of the *semantic component* of the language. Language development cannot be thought of except in essential relation to the structure of experience. Every community has sets of things, events, values and features of experience that the growing and maturing individual has to somehow undergo and confront. Language from another perspective is a *representative symbolic system* of the totality of the cultural and social experiences of a community. As such a mastery over this symbolic system, or rather an acquaintance with the system means an internalisation of the features of experience in terms of sets of abstractions which we may call concepts. As the child progresses in language, in a parallel manner, as language learning is not a process of committing linguistic items to memory, he more and more internalises the semantics of the language in the form of meanings and meaning specifications resulting in a continuous acquaintance with the cultural and sociological aspects of the community. In short the entire process of language learning is one of *internalisation of systems* : phonological, morphological (vocabulary), symtactic and semantic systems of the language.

5. Acquiring the Phonology of L_1

The first and the basic linguistic system which the child internalises, as we have seen in the foregoing pages, is the phonology of the language. Constant acquaintance with adult language enables the child to increase his sound-stock. Internalisation is not a compartmentalised process in terms of the systems. It is not that the child takes in the entire sound system of the particular language and then goes on to acquire the vocabulary of the language. It is more of an overlapping process with the result that each system goes more or less parallel to others. The child produces more or less 'non-distinctive' sounds during the random articulation-phase. At the same time the child's ears are constantly fed with *adult-language* produced at varying situations at home. As all this language consists of sounds which are definable in terms of this phonetic characteristics, the child's auditory organs get acquainted with these and in course of time, as a result, the random articulation is substituted by the sounds of the language. In itself it is a gradual process and takes years before the major portion of the sounds are mastered exactly. While the acquisition of the sounds is in progress, the child is in a position, already to comprehened words, and even phrases. This is why it is impossible to demarcate the beginning and end of any one process.

The sounds produced by man to give shape to his language have unique features. They are very different from the sounds, produced in the cries of birds and animals. It has not yet been shown if the cry of an animal (*e.g.* the chattering of monkeys) consists of definable sound units and a recombination of these is ever possible to these animals. The same is true of the cries of birds. These are all set, stereotyped order of sounds which do not permit any change in its usual sequence. But in case of man it is otherwise, p, b, k, g, t or d are sound units of English Language. It is a fact that requires no description that 'n' number of combinations of these sounds with the other sounds of the language are possible. A reordering of these sounds results in a variety of words in the language. This is how language has become possible at all. This *reorganisation* of sounds into varieties of sequential forms is possible only with human language. This is possible because the sounds produced by man in the production of language are physically, definable in terms of the *features* of *articulation*.

At the stage of random articulation the infant produces the sounds da.....da.....da.....da..... We have explained it as a vocal-ear reflex. But when the mother holds out a doll and says *doll* the 'da........da.........' sounds assume a special role. From a *non-distinctive level* these sounds are elevated to the level of *distinctive sounds* of the language and as a result the child now produces *do.......do.......do.......* sounds with a two-pronged correspondence. The /dɔ:/ sounds on the one hand correspond to and are the result of the random articulation da.......da.......da.......da......., and on the other, the unit corresponds to the word *doll* produced by the mother. At the present stage it is not possible for the infant to imitate the word doll; but the sounds which stand out in the word are assimilated by and are made part of the child's language.

The same happens with other phonological elements of the language. As the child's experience with adult language increases, the stock of sounds acquired thus is found to increase. In a continuous but involuntary endeavour to pick up one's own language, the native child masters one sound after another in the context of his language behaviour. But the process is so long and tedious that at the beginning very few sounds may be pronounced exactly eventhough semi-nonsense words are structured during the first stage. Whatever sound units and sequences of sounds are mastered are employed in words of some kind *i.e.* semi-nonsense words. It happens in such cases that perhaps only the mother knows what the child utters sometimes and asks for. It may be altogether unintelligible to others.

6. Acquiring the Vocabulary of L_1

The earliest forms uttered by the child employing the distinctive sounds which he has picked up, are non-sense words which have partial similarity to those produced by the elders.

These are usually heard in the form of 'unc' for uncle, 'en' for hen, 'mik' for milk 'do' for doll and so on. This partial resemblance enables the elders to recognize what the child utters together with the situation in which the form is produced. A characteristic thing of this period is that while producing words of partial resemblance, the child at the same time is in a position to recognize a few hundred words which he cannot actively produce. This again helps the child establish contact with the grown up of the family. It shows that the forms of these words are some how internalized, acquired, by the child while immaturity of the articulatory organs in giving shape to the sequences hinders the child from actively producing these forms.

Individual differences affect the mastery over the forms of language as it happens in all aspects of development. Constitutional as well as environmental differences, the potency for cognitive organization, opportunities for learning and practising and a large number of related factors influence the intensity of picking up words from the language the child listens to every day.

The presence of synonyms, antonyms, homophones, idioms and proverbial uses in the language of the adults cause problems for the child. Contrast and comparison form one of the basic processes with which the child picks up the *vocabulary* of the language. These occurs in day-to-day life similar or identical situations from which through contrast and comparison the child deducts both morphological aspects and vocabulary. This, again, is intensified by the use of *analogy* by the child. Traditionally analogy has been given the greatest role in language learning process. The child who is habituated to the forms *walking-walked, moving-moved* and *proving-proved* produces with confidence forms like *going-goed* Here the child is said to employ the principle of analogy. The constant recurrence of a word helps the child pick up the form and at the same time contrasts the same in the production of another word in another situation. *Drink water, drink tea* and *drink milk* make the child produce an utterance like *drink food* where he goes wrong. Here the adult interferes to correct him.

The constant familiarity with forms like : *walks, walking* and *walked, moves, moving* and *moved, names, naming* and *named*, and *looks, looking* and *looked* helps the child distinguish morphemes such as : –s, –ing and –ed as some sort of separate units. Thereby the child will attempt the use of the same with word forms where he goes wrong. It is certainly not the mistake of the child, but of the language in which exceptions to a rule are too many.

In the process of acquiring new words the child is required to fix *semantic limits, distinctions* and *restrictions*. It is a type of *contextual analysis* to isolate words and to recognize their senses. This is a process of demarcating the boundaries of linguistic units at various levels starting from sounds to semantics. The acquisition of the vocabulary of L_1 is governed, again, by the principles of simplicity, usefulness, proximity, particularity and concreteness. Words with these characteristics are always acquired earlier than their opposits in various degrees. The child is bound to learn a word like *bed* much earlier than *cushion* or *school*. The vocabulary which the child acquires is related first to his physiological needs, things and experiences of the family circle, experiences of the neighbourhood and then further it extends to world outside until it subsumes in a gradual manner the lexicon of the language he grows up to use as an adult.

7. Acquiring the Syntax of L_1

The process of internalization reaches its peak in the acquisition of the *syntax* of the language. Acquiring the basic syntax of the language is something stretched along from the beginning of the language learning process until the child is said to reach what is known as 'linguistic adulthood' around the age of six. The internalization of the grammar of the language, in fact, begins when the child comprehends the sentences constructed by the adults. The chief function associated with the *acquisition of syntax* is the ordering of word-elements in a sentence. From the production of non-sense utterances the child progresses to individual but correct words. But the most interesting thing is that the individual, linguistically isolated words uttered by the child are no longer semantically isolated at this stage. So to say, the isolated words are full, frozen and condensed expressions surging out of the child's maturing mind. Looking at a picture when the child utters the word apple it is a full-fledged sentence in the form of *it is an apple* frozen into the single word 'apple'. The same happens with utterances such as *water, go, me* or *mama*, the mother who is utmost conscious of the child's needs finds no difficulty in recognizing these utterances chiefly because the child places these utterances in various *contextual setting* which enables the mother to understand the utterances as : *I need water, you go away from me, give me the doll* and *please, hold me in your arms, mama*. All these are condensed into semantically compressed one-word utterances as given above.

This certainly shows that the child at this stage is able at least to recognize utterances of the above kind produced by the adults. More and more he acquires the basic patterns of the sentences of the native language with the result that in course of time communication through *phrases* and further through *short sentences* become possible on the basis of the patterns that are already internalized. In the context of *transformational generative grammar*, the factor mentioned above is the *linguistic competence* of the child the building blocks of which have been discussed in the foregoing pages. The essence of competence is the internalized linguistic systems, not only syntax in the restricted sense, but the manifold *systems of the language* beginning with the sounds to the meanings.

Linguistic competence is the 'generator' of the sentences of the native language. The acquisition of the sound system, and the vocabulary enables the child to organize the entire linguistic material he listens to in terms of the *basic patterns* of his language. As a result the child builds up a 'generator' *i.e.* the complex syntactic system as the resource of all the language that he is going to produce in future. A basic pattern of English such as : *I walk*, as part of the linguistic competence of the child, enables the child later to produce at the surface level sentences such as :

I walk
He walks
They walk
I am walking
You are walking
He has walked
You have walked etc.

With the internalization of each pattern, the child becomes capable of structuring 'n' number of sentences within the same pattern as the need arises. Thus the '*syntactic spectrum*' in the child's brain functions like a generator enabling the speaker to produce sentences *i.e.* correct sentences as per the patterns that make up the tautum of the 'syntactic spectrum'. Any discrepancy in the formation of these patterns results in the production of wrong sentences. With the L_1 learner this does not happen as no such structure is formally taught; all that he picks up are by means of a *process* of *abstraction* from the structures produced by the adult speakers of the language. The result of such an abstraction are the *phrase-structure rules* considered basic to the transformational generative process.

8. The Process of Socialization and Acquisition of Semantic Maturity

The development of language and the process of socialization go so much hand in hand that both lead towards what may be called *Semantic maturity*. The beginning of language development takes place in a highly egocentric context. As we have seen the child is the centre of a world of experiences, and these experiences are *centrifugal* in terms of the child. The earliest material which the child masters are of egocentric nature; he picks up words only for those things that satisfy his earliest biological needs and later of things that belong to his socio-physical surroundings such as the things around and the people at home. All these elements are expected to satisfy the child's requirements in varied manner. It takes three or four years before the child begins picking up words for actual socializing *paralinguistic experiences*. The earliest pronouns are centered on as well as directed to the self; the use of *we*, *us*, *our*, *they* etc. come only much later.

Real growth of language can seldom be separated from *socialization*. Socialization may be viewed as a process in which the child at first becomes aware of the presence of 'the others', and accept 'the others' as part of his experiences. It is a movement from the self to the world at large enveloping and involving others in society in the world of the self instead of more and more becoming isolated from society. It is a widening of the individual's horizon from the narrow circle of the ego to an all embracing vision of humanity.

Language is not an isolated system in the abstract. No natural language is isolated from a given society. Every language is, in other words, representative of the *socio-cultural experiences* of a community. Consequently, if language is such, the development *i.e.* acquisition of language with the socio-cultural components of the particular community. Although one may visualize an abstract, isolated and away from learning of a language by a foreign student, yet even in this context what the individual is not acquainted with are only those aspects of the people's life which are strange to and different from the native way of life. This can never be the case with the L_1 learner who is wholly immersed in the experiences of the native community and there is no escape from it in normal circumstances.

Learning the language, against the background given above, means an *accumulation* of greater semantic facts parallel to the accumulation of the vocabulary and expressions of the language. The proverbs, idioms, and varied expressions peculiar to the native language are the *Semantic carriers* specific to the language apart from the meaning specifications that represents the ordinary experiences of the community such as related to family life, religions life, experiences of school, those of the peer group and further of later friend circles as well as those of professional life.

As the individual's experiences widen and acquaintance with the reality of life increases, language too matures in a parallel manner. The end-result is what we called earlier, a *Semantic maturity* which essentially links language with the socio-cultural experiences. It can well be considered part of the individual's personality development, as semantic maturity means the broadening of the world-vision of the individual. At this level it is easy for us to find how essentially the language of a community and the individual's personality development are linked. In other words, *socialization*, as an essential aspect of the development of personality is directly linked with the development of the native language.

3
Approaches to Language Teaching

1. The Role of Language Theories

At any time in the history of language teaching, teachers have never been on their own. The teacher whether in informal or formal teaching situations took directions from those who spoke authoritatively on language. Inquiry into the nature of human language was an element common to all the philosophers of the earliest known times. The most modern linguists are not different from the earliest philosophers in regard to one thing: the purposes of *investigations* into the *phenomenon of language*. Such investigations have always had two objects: (1) A disinterested enquiry into the nature of human language for the sake of objective knowledge; and (2) on the basis of whatever knowledge is obtained, the method of teaching a language is organized. The aims are not different today and they will not be different as long as such enquiries will continue although never new dimensions will be added. The language teacher is not expected to be a theoretician and possess all insights into language and its functioning. The teacher depends on the researches undertaken and the theoretical pronouncements of language specialists such as linguist or a psycho or socio-linguist who are on the continual trail of the complex phenomenon of language. The beginning is the theoretician: the linguist, psychologist, sociologist or educationist; and the end is the *teacher* who functions as the actual classroom practitioner on whom the learner depends. Between both the ends: the theoretician and the teacher, the theories are concretized, structured and restructured so as to give shape to various language teaching *methods* which will in turn yield the actual classroom *techniques* for the functioning of the teacher in class. In other word language theories function as the remote guidelines for the teacher's approach to the teaching of the foreign language.

2. Behaviourism in Psychology

All contemporary psychological approaches to language boils down to two fundamental sets of theories: (1) *Behaviourist* theories of language, and (2) *Cognitive* theories of language. Both the schools have variations in themselves, but the fundamental assumptions of the sub-theories are the same. The Behaviourist and cognitive schools of psychology aim at a functional explanation of language learning, but both offer divergent answers to the problem of the formation of language habits. The behaviourist believes that learning is basically a process of conditioning. A series of connected stimulus response bonds (situations) lead the learner to the desired goal in learning. Learning takes place in the connection between the *stimulus* and the associated *response*. When the learner, thus, as a result of conditioning, can give the desired response, we say, he has learned. It may be said that a person's *learned behaviours* consist of countless conditioned responses. In this thoroughly mechanistic approach the behaviourist conceives language learning as conditioned verbal behaviour consisting of a series of stimulus-response bonds. As we have examined it, the core of language learning is the formation of a set of language habits which consists of conditioned responses. These habits can only be formed by making the learner spend a major part of his time responding to the specific stimuli, in otherwords, practising the patterns. *Repetition* is the key to the formation of language habits in the present context. The entire work consists of automatic and non-thoughtful responses to the set stimuli, which is a thoroughly mechanical process. In the first half of the twentieth century, especially in the 30's and 40's we find behaviourism greatly influencing linguistics and the entire field of language teaching. On the basis of the conditioning process, bulks of programmed instructional material began to appear.

Skinner's own 'learning frames' for programmed instruction consist of conditioned responses based on the principle of conditioning, which received wide acceptance. In short learning in behaviourist psychology is a *process of conditioning*, and not a process of the mind which is expected to entertain knowledge at all levels.

3. Cognitivism in Psychology

The cognitive school of psychology has in recent years, quite a contrary explanation to offer. The intense adherence to behaviourist principles has already been declining and there is in present day psychology and linguistics a resurrection, so to say, of the fascinating roles of the *mind* which alone explains the phenomena of language, knowledge and thought process. The learner, in the cognitive context, is thought of as possessing a cognitive structure into which any new learning is subsumed. Language learning in the last resort is the function of the *cognitive structure* of the individual learner. The entire cognitive interpretation of language learning rests upon the neuro-psychological (by contrast to neuro-muscular) bases of thought. and for this matter cognitive theories are at times called mentalistic. Learning is thought of as acquisition and storage of knowledge in and through the cognitive structure of the individual, which is the neuro-psychological substratum of though process. Unlike the behaviourists who explains language learning purely as a *mechanistic process*, for cognitive psychology language learning is a '*meaningful process*.' Learning consists in understanding, on the one hand, and on the other relating the new material to the previous experiences of the learner for whom all learning is a 'thoughtful process.'

Just as 'structuralism in linguistics' beginning with Leonard Bloomfield, derived its basic assumptions from behaviourism, the cognitive school of psychology is the chief parallel to transformational generative grammar which considers language learning as a rule-governed behaviour' rather than a conditioning process. Language was thought of as a rule-governed behaviour involving the cognitive faculties of man, by the traditional grammars and by the medieval schools of philosophy. But Noam Chomsky in 1957 and later gave a fresh and formal touch to this aspect of language learning and brought about a whole trend in linguistics known today as *transformational generative grammar*. The characteristics features of transformationalism will be dealt with in Section 5. The two schools in psychology have had distinct impacts on contemporary thinking in linguistics. The skinnerian 'connectionism' has been the last phase of behaviourist psychology which explained language in terms of operant conditioning. For over three decades before the 1950's, descriptive linguistics followed the strict foot-paths of behaviourism; this school of linguistics which adhered to the assumptions of behaviourist psychology is known today a structuralism. On the one hand behaviourist psychology directly, and on the other, structuralist linguistics controlled the foreign language teaching methodologies; and the impact of this influence is so great that present-day language teaching practices still adhere to structuralist principles.

4. Structuralism in Linguistics

The first half of the twentieth century witnessed a constant shift from functionalism to structuralism both in psychology and in linguistics, and something which influenced all sciences for that matter. The functional views of mentalism traditionally hold received several setbacks due to the ever-increasing influence of Darvin's theory of evolution and allied facts. The basic assumption was that reality structured and that structure may be predicted of reality and expressed as a set of elements holding a fixed set of relationships. This approach to reality which is held as invariably amenable to investigation (unlike the mental realities and presuppositions in mentalism), was a basic proposition of all behavioural sciences; the aim at the period was to make modern linguistics a thoroughly behavioural science and lead the science of language away from the clutches of mentalist presuppositions. Leonard Bloomfield's works on language brought this approach on its focus for the first time. Bloomfield wanted to raise linguistics to the level of any other behavioural science such as the physical sciences which exclusively depend on experimentation for their results and development. It was chiefly due to Bloomfield that structuralism assumed a definite shape in linguistics. Many consider Ferdinand Saussure a Swiss linguist as the initiator of structuralism in linguistics. But Leonard Bloomfield's 'Language' (1933) was the clear structuralist landmark in linguistics.

The fundamental structuralist assumption, thus, is that language is a *structured system* of components with set relationships that may be differentiated by the analyst. The linguist's endeavour is to study the structure of the language by isolating the units of the languages and by establishing the correct relationships among them. Language here is almost identified with its structures and their relationships. The functional and the operational factors of language are not taken care of by the structuralists. There are several other features that characterised structuralism in linguistics. Language is thought of primarily as *speech*; and for all purposes of fundamental research only the spoken form of language is used as the data. The priority given to speech affected all aspects of language analysis. There came a transition from the traditionalists' preoccupation with written language, mainly literary works, to the structuralists' emphasis on the actual language spoken in a community. It was, consequently, a transition from prescriptivism to *descriptivism*. While traditional grammars aimed at presenting a body of analytical material in terms of sets of rules to be followed by the speakers or learners of the language, and even native speakers were required to adhere to the sets of rules, structuralist linguistics, due to its insights into the role of the changing and evolving forms of spoken language studied the language of a *given people* at a *given period* and described the language as used by the people. This was indeed a very major shift in grammatical approach: the transition from traditional prescriptivism to modern *descriptive linguistics*. The scientific value and validity of structuralist approach, as claimed, lie in its direct access to the living and changing language of the speech community observed and collected as the primary data for linguistic analysis.

The initial work of the structural linguists principally centered around the phonological component of language *i.e.*, the study of the sound system. As language is conceived of as a system structured of identifiable components or levels, the structuralists posited a number of levels in language: (1) phonology, (2) Morphology, (3) Syntax and (4) Semantics. The 1930s for structural linguistics was a decade of *phonology*, and the 1940s and the first half of 1950s a period of intense concentration on *Morphology* It is the 1960s, the Chomskyan period, that is considered the decade of *Syntax* when the study of syntax is intensely pursued. But the structuralists are not accredited with the pursuit of syntax as by the 1960s Transformationalism became the fashion of the day. The structuralist analysis seldom got beyond phonology and morphology; the interest in real theory-building was little. Even in phonology and morphology, the major contribution was towards the analysis of the phonological and morphological structure of particular languages. The study of these linguistic components was not undertaken within any unified theoritical frame-work except that contributed mainly by Bloomfield.

But structuralism received wide acceptance in linguistic circles as the aims were moderate, concrete and it professed non adherence to any mentalist notions. Its strict adherence to the behaviourist traits has had obvious results in applied linguistics such as foreign language teaching methods. Structuralist principles along with experimental linguistics had much to offer towards more efficient instruction and objective evaluation. Presuppositions have no place in structuralism; this attitude maintained its thoroughly scientific nature and it helped linguistics for a long while from getting entangled with psychological and philosophical problems which used to be essentially attached to language. The principal drawback of structuralism is its very narrow linguistic scope and limited theoretical concerns.

5. Transformationalism in Linguistics

In Noam Chomsky (1957) we have the onset of transformational generative approach to the study of language. The onset of *transformationalism* is an important landmark in the history of linguistics. By this period structuralist ideas have already got deep-rooted in the field of foreign language teaching methodology. Transformationalism came into linguistics with the traditional but highly refined and refreshed message of creativity, inventiveness and 'mentalism' (with due regard for the role of the mind in language acquisition and production). Language, for the transformationalist, is fundamentally a creative and generative process. After decades of exclusive emphasis of linguistic structure, the functional aspects of human language received attention again in transformationalism. Language is not the result of large-scale imitation, trial and error or stimulus-response bonds, but it is considered that creativity pervades all aspects of language.

Language is basically conceived at its depth-level, the *Semantic Component* being the material for language to work on at this deeper level. Meanings are outlaid at the semantic component of language, a level which has not become so much the object of the strict transformational description. The transformationalist attention has been focussed on syntax as the basis of language competence against the background of the semantic component. In the study of syntax, transformationalism does not adhere to strict observation as in the behaviourist-oriented structuralism. Transformationalism claims that there is greater and deeper patterning to language than what could be derived from a set of superficial data, because for the transformationalist language is more abstract and has more introspective elements than would be agreed upon by the structuralist. The pre-eminence of the semantic component of language in the linguistic structure is realized later by a set of semanticists in 1960s and 1970s, within the fold of transformational generative grammar. This will be examined in the following section.

Transformationalism retains the view of *language-as-knowledge* and the actual use of the language, speech or writing, in the distinction between 'competence and performance.' The native child with his continual exposure to and acquaintence with his language in course of years internalizes the linguistic system and develops the basic competence of his language. The condition for the internalization of the language is the exposure to the language atmosphere. There is a deeper 'take in' process happening in the child during this exposure than would be posited by the superficial stimulus-responds connections. The child is a human person interacting with his social environment and guided by his basic creative intelligence he masters the language. The competence build-up by means of internalization now functions, as the substratum for 'linguistic creativity' which makes transformationalism unique among the theories of language. The native child or the L_1 learner of English, in other words, produces sentences which he has never heard before or he himself has never produced before. It is the basic linguistic inventiveness, creativity, that enables him to produce such ever new combinations of the words of the language. The child has the potency, thus for producing an infinite set of sentences based on a finite set of words. The items of the lexicon of the language are finite in number included in a dictionary of the language; but none can ever list the complete possible set of sentences which can be constructed using all the words listed in the lexicon of the language. Here lies the creative characteristic of human language as well as of the speaker.

If the structuralist treated the learner in the classroom as an organism not in any way better than the animal which can be easily conditioned to a given mechanical bond, the learner for the transformationalist, is a creatively potent individual whose behaviour is *rule-governed*, purposeful and orderly, as well as controlled not only by superficial neuromuscular factors but also principally by a 'centre' in the human personality-structure. Eventhough transformational generative grammar is not intended directly for purposes of classroom-practice, the fundamentals of this linguistic theory are so potent and appealing to enhance classroom practices that it has come to have great bearing on present day thinking in this direction. The child is no longer to be considered a sheer organism to be manipulated under controlled situations; the child picks up the language by means of internalization in a thoroughly language atmosphere through continuous exposure to the language used around. A few isolated patterns with which practice is provided in the classroom are not the whole of the language. The real flesh of the language, its varies uses and applications can be mastered by the child only if the child is exposed to the language as a unified phenomenon. Language is not mainly a set of habits to be picked up. It is knowledge, competence, and this knowledge can be internalized only by means of a unified approach to language in which more and more chances are provided in the classroom and outside for the learner to learn language as a *creative experience* which appeals to all his mental and physiological faculties of language.

6. Semanticism in Linguistics

Within the tradition of transformational generative grammar, in recent years, there has come up the most recent development in Linguistics which we may know as '*Semanticism.*' Semanticism designates the trend in Linguistics which places emphasis above all on the semantic component of language. Semanticism even goes to the extend of saying that the whole of linguistic investigation in truth consists in the study of semantics. As we have seen, structuralism placed emphasis on or could investigate only into the phonological and later the morphological components of language. Transformationalism which came after saw linguistics primarily from the viewpoint of syntax and focussed all attention on the study of syntax in an attempt to make up for the syntactic deficiencies of earlier phases. Reacting to Noam Chomsky's theoretical standpoints in regard to the deep-structure—Surface structure differences and to the semantic role exclusively assigned to the deep structure, Some Linguistists felt that a compartmentalization of syntax and semantics as has been done in linguistics would not solve any relevant problems. They felt that the foremost problems to be solved are those of semantics and that syntax is not a component of language separable from semantics.

Those who held such a viewpoint in the 1960's and 1970's are Weinreich, George Lakoff, James Macawley, Kuroda, Jackendoff etc. These semanticists felt that all questions in linguistics chiefly boil down to two fundamental questions: (1) What are the regularistics that govern and which linear sequences of words and morphemes of a language are permitted and which are not? (2) what are the regularities by which the surface forms (sounds) are paired with this meanings? Transformational generative grammar saw the two questions as different and attempted an answer to the first without answering the second. But semanticists like George Lakoff pointed out that the two questions above are not essentially different and that the two questions (one pertaining to syntax and other to semantics) must be answered simultaneously without giving syntactic questions precedence over semantic questions. This position has come to be known as 'Generative Semantics' named after the title of the work, ' Generative Semantics' by George Lakoff.

Semanticism is in fact a healthy revival of the age-old cry for the legitimate recognition of the *meaning component* of human language. Meanings in language received almost a death-blow in the hands of the 20th century bahavicurists, the progeny of traditional materialism. The structuralist linguists after Leonard Bloomfield held an aversin for meanings except for heuristic purposes; and meanings had no entry into any level of linguistic analysis.

With no longer any fear in the minds of linguists in regard to the recognition of the role of the human mind in language acquisition and performance, *meanings* have again come to receive due attention. Present day linguistics has taken upon itself the challenge of investigating into the linguistic structure of meanings. It is a movement from the superficial linguistic components to the deepest aspects of language. The progress of semanticism is bound to boost language study and consequently foreign language teaching methods. As it has often been emphasized in structuralism, transformationalism and in semanticism, linguistic investigations principally aim at only one thing: the regularistics of relationships between the component of sound and the component of meanings. For the human child and the common native speaker language means precisely this: the way to express this *inner world of thoughts* in terms of *sound sequences*. Language for the child is not syntax or morphology, but experiences, meanings, communication and behaviour. The Socio-cultural implications of meanings make their structure more complex than visualized by the universalists of the middle ages. Had language been sounds and grammar only, an abstract treatment of the same would teach the language. But learning a new language requires that the individual has to assimilate a different culture.

7. Approach Method and Techniques

Clarity is required as to how exactly one may differentiate between approaches, methods and techniques. Knowledge of these relevant aspects of teaching is essential for the teacher in view of the need to equip himself for the organisation of his classroom practices. The teacher is an individual who is put in the classroom situation and is expected to play certain set of roles. In course of his classroom practices which are a set of interactions with his pupils, the teacher performs a number of related activities. These activities are the component elements of the teacher's overall behaviour in the classroom. In otherword the teacher's behaviour in the classroom consists of component acts each of which can be of two kinds: (1) a disorganized and haphazard set of acts without essential and well-intended relatedness among the component acts, and (2) an organized, sequential and fully related set of acts each of which is intended to serve some specified purpose. These component units of the teacher's behaviour in the classroom, we shall call *techniques*. But any teacher behaves in the classroom and organizes the teaching activities in accordance to a set of proximate principles which are either the teacher's own mental construct or are based on recommendations by experts. These proximate principles or guidelines we may call, *methods*. Again, the proximate guidelines in regard to the class practices are directly linked to two factors: (1) the teacher's own understanding of an insights into the nature of language, the child and of classroom practices themselves; and (2) theories which are directly intended to highlight classroom practices in general language teaching in particular. These comparatively remote principles and theories which on the one hand highlight the language behaviour in the classroom, and on the other indirectly control the teacher's classroom performance are known as *approaches*. Farther than the approaches, there are factors which exercise control over the teacher's work in the classroom; in fact the approaches to the teaching of a foreign language themselves are controlled by what we may call basic *theories on language* which as such have nothing to do with language teaching in the classroom, instead, are concerned about the basic nature of language and human behaviour.

Thus we have been able to trace a whole hierarchy of factors which influence and determine the actual work by the teacher in the classroom. *Techniques* being the most concrete units of behaviour in the classroom are controlled by *methods* and these in turn are determined by *approaches* to the teaching of foreign languages. The approaches further are determined by the *theories on language* which may be psychological theories or linguistic theories. Such theories provide the ultimate framework and guidelines for the functioning of the teacher in the classroom. But as these basic theories are very remote to the classroom, one may conjoin the approaches and the theories of language for practical purposes under one head: Approaches. Thus we may further say, in other words, that approaches are principles or axioms which remotely guide the teacher's awareness and organization of his work in the classroom *i.e. Approaches* are *axiomatic* by nature and being abstract conceptual organization or theory, the teacher may or may not be conscious of them. *Methods* are *procedural* in the sense that they outlay in proximate and more concrete manner the overall functioning of the teacher in the classroom: *Techniques* are *implementational* in the sense, as we have seen them, that techniques are the actual units of the teacher's behaviour in the classroom. They are sets of teaching devices which the teacher employs at every stage of his teaching practice and through which he implements the principles and guidelines laid out by the methods proximately and an Approach remotely.

8. Foreign Language Teaching Methods

Language theories are the foundation from which foreign language teaching methods are formulated and derived. The beginning of the present chapter shows that there are quite a number of theories which have formed the very foundations for the current language teaching methods. *Behaviourism, Cognitivism, Structuralism, Transformationalism* and *Semanticism* have been examined as the fundamental theories on language some of which have helped derive remarkable methods for the teacher of L_2 while others are influencing the present-day language teaching practices. The following chapter examines how the medieval understanding of grammar as a universal phenomenon (what is known as 'Universal Grammar') gave rise to the *grammar-translation method* which held the reins as the only teaching method for centuries together. It is sometimes acclaimed as the 'Universal Methods' of foreign language teaching. The medieval scholastic theories of language provided the fundamental principles of grammar translation method.

The onset of behaviourism in psychology and subsequently structuralism in linguistics came as a reaction to the 'mentalist presuppositions' which had influenced psychology and language studies. The theory of universal grammar came to be thoroughly disgusting to the structuralists. The whole approach to language received new dimensions in the hands of the structuralists. Human language which had been a '*mental structure*' with the philosophers and the grammarians came to be something dynamic and laudably alive. The role of grammarians received a tilt in the hands of the structuralists. Grammar became the organisational relations of the language spoken by the living community rather than the abstractions based on the classical works in literature. This indeed was a significa[illegible] major change in viewpoint that could be considered a landmark in the history of language study. The spirit of structuralism came to be at once felt in the area of foreign language teaching at a time when language teaching received the most acute attention *i.e.* between the two World Wars, and especially during the post-war period. What are today known as structural approach and audio-lingual approach are the direct results of the applications of the principles of structuralism in the teaching of foreign languages.

If structuralism in Linguistics is directly linked to structural approach and audio-lingual approach to the teaching of foreign languages, there arose a codified method which could be again described as a sharp antithesis to grammar-translation method. This foreign language teaching method is the *direct method.* Direct method with its emphasis of spoken language and direct association between language and features of experience without the medium of the mother-tongue is directly related to the theoretical formulations of structuralism.

Among the methods which attempts a formulation of the classroom procedures by the teacher the most prominent ones are the following: grammar-translation method, direct method, Michael West's reading method, and Dodson's bilingual method. In fact everyone of the foreign language teaching methods mentioned here has had an evolutionary history of its own. It is only that in the hands of a theoretician these methods received formal initiation. The teacher systematically attempting to work with a language in the classroom somehow falls within one or other of the methods mentioned above, or his method will come out to be more or less of an eccelectical nature having made use of the best in every method. The teacher's functioning in the classroom can be effective and the units of his classroom behaviour fully and systematically related only when he functions within the framework of some method. The best method for that matter is one that the teacher himself evolves in an ecclectical manner on the basis of his classroom experiences and suited best to the situation in which he works.

9. Teaching Techniques and the Classroom

The foreign language teaching guidelines become more abstract and axiomatic as we move away from the classroom, and assume more concrete dimensions as we get closer to the classroom. The conceptual organization in the minds of the theoretician becomes dynamic instruments of language teaching in the hands of the teacher. The life-less lines of the book become the living pulses of the classroom in the form of teaching techniques. Techniques are tools in the hands of the teacher by the use of which the teacher obtains interaction with the pupils. The more organized and sequentially related these tools are, the better will be the *teaching-learning process.*

The teaching techniques which may be employed in the teaching of L_2 and varied and are skill and component specific (See Mukalel & Shabbir Ahmed, 1984). Every method mentioned in the preceding section consists of techniques which either are unique to the methods or are new organisation of traditional techniques. One of the most resourceful language teaching technique is *questioning* which is not a unique invention of any one method. Questioning which is a technique which is quite naturally at the disposal of the teacher for effective interaction, will form part of any teaching method. Questioning as a technique has place both in the grammar-translation method as well as in the direct method, the two polarities of foreign language teaching methods which are diametrically opposed. But a technique such as 'dramatization' or 'miming' doesn't form part of all methods as the features of dramatization are befitting only in the context of the direct methods where a direct relationship is established between language and experience.

Techniques, in this manner, are units of behaviour or aspects of the teacher's activities which are to a great extent definable themselves. As tools in the hands of the teacher, they are independent and can be manipulated as the teacher wishes. But under the guidelines of every methods the techniques are organized and reorganized to create the learning effect as required by the basic principles of the particular method. The uniqueness and features characteristic to any one teaching method, thus, do not lie with the techniques themselves but which the way the techniques (traditional or newly introduced) one sequentially organized for purposes of creating the learning effect required by the particular teaching method. For this reason the ultimate success of any teaching method depends on the creative ability of the teacher.

10. The Basic Need for Methodology

There are those who argue that no methods are necessary for an efficient teacher. The contradiction involved in this argument is self-evident. No teacher, it is evident, can do without some method. Method doesnot mean or is it identical with grammar-translation method or bilingual method. The language teacher as a classroom practitioner requires to employ some systematic approach to the teaching of the language. The effectiveness of the teacher's work in the classroom and the overall fruits he will reap will depend on the efficiency of his approach. The more *systematic* and *scientific* his approach to the classroom is, the better will be the effectiveness in terms of language learning. Those who argue that a *creative teacher* needs no methods commit the fallacy of contradiction in that the creative imagination of the teacher helps him organize his classroom behaviour so much that a method of his own is the outcome. In fact, any educationist would agree a teaching method evolved out of the varied experiences of the teacher incorporating the best out of several methods and suiting to the particular situation is the best method.

The theories of language, approaches to language teaching, and methods of teaching foreign languages will remain unproductive and abstract so long as these principles and guidelines do not generate in the classroom techniques which are the only teaching devices beneficial to language teaching in the last resort. The language teacher with creative imagination and resourcefulness as well as a deep sensitivity to the linguistic needs of his pupils organizes the classroom techniques that are known to him, employs those news introduced to him and endeavours to find for himself teaching techniques which are adequate enough to meet his objectives in the classroom. In such an attempt to meet the language teaching requirements, the resourceful teacher rises above the horizons of any one method and by organizing his teaching techniques in new ways gives effect to teaching methods of his own.

No method recommends every little details that the teacher has to do in class. Methods consist mostly of guidelines that are broad and provide a framework for the organizing the teacher's behaviour in the classroom. The gaps and the freedom which any method permits are indeed a healthy sign so that a creative and resourceful teacher has a role of his own to play and original contributions to make within the outline of the method. Language proficiency and thoughtful approach to the method one employs are basic requirements for the successful teaching of a language. The officially recognized method is only a raw material at the teacher's disposal, which need be suitably employed in the classroom by means of creative thinking on the part of teacher. There are no wholesale methods which the teacher may be able to use without employing his own mind and originality. Any method, for that matter, requires the teacher's final polishing touch and organisation to be come adequate for the use in the class room. The final result of the language learning experiences in the classroom is governed by the way the teacher employs the method.

4
Grammar-Translation Method

1. The Basic Principles

Of all the second or foreign language teaching methods, *grammar-translation method* took the longest period of time to evolve finally into almost a universal foreign language teaching method. It has been so universal, and its impact so great and lasting that even today *grammar-translation method* survives in various forms in all parts of the world. A chapter is dedicated to treat the grammar-translation method only because of its tremendous universal appeal. As the very name reveals, it is a foreign language teaching method which consists exclusively of the formal teaching of grammar, and translation from and to the mother-tongue of the learner. Grammar-translation method had a natural evolution all over the world and no one is known to be the initiator of such a method. Some of the fundamental assumptions which worked behind the evolution of grammar-translation method could be stated as follows: (1) Language proper is its *written forms* and no care was taken to study the spoken language as part of the enquiry into the nature of language. (2) Languages are fundamentally *universal*. Languages boil down to a fundamental set of universal concepts which are expressed by means of various forms in different languages. (3) All languages have fundamentally the same grammar. Apart from the superficial differences in grammar, the same grammar explains the basic features of all languages. (4) Contrast by the grammar of the mother-tongue will enable the learner to master the grammar of the foreign language. *Translation* is considered the best device to achieve such a grammatical contrast. (5) The patterns of the foreign language are learned by translation of material from and to the mother-tongue. (6) A *formal* learning of the rules of L_2 grammar by contrast to those of the L_1 grammar helps the learner to master the language. Therefore the learning of the grammar consists in learning the rules of the grammar.

Based on assumptions such as above grammar-translation method taught the foreign language through the processes of translation and formal teaching of the grammar of the language. It is helpful to understand the working of the grammar-translation method if we examine the above assumptions more in detail. Before European Renaissance brought about a change in the attitude towards national and regional languages, all that the Europeans could think of teaching in educational institutions were the *classical languages* of Greek and Latin. In fact the word language was almost identified with the classical languages, so much so that any person deemed to be educated had to be well-versed in the disciplines of Latin and Greek. In contemporary India too education primarily meant the learning of *Sanskrit*, as the reading of the scriptures presupposed the knowledge of Sanskrit. The principal motivations for language learning during the middle ages both in Europe and in India were the same: the reading and the study of the *scriptures* and the classical writings. As education and learning in Europe were controlled primarily by Christian institutions, and in India by Brahmnistic sects, there was an exclusive concentration especially during the middle ages, on the Bible and the classical writings in Europe, and on the Sacred Scriptures and other works in Sanskrit in India. As learning was geared to the understanding of these works, the only logical method which would evolve out of all attempts to teach the scriptures and the classical works was a concentration on reading and writing. It came to be that both in India and in Europe the earliest teaching methods were centred on enabling the child to read the sacred books, and *read* and *write* in the classical languages although in India the Brahministic traditions initially taught the memorized recitation of the sacred verses and the child in course of time learned reading the verses. Such is the history behind the exclusive emphasis of reading and writing, and it is the rationale behind the evolution of the whole grammar-translation method in India and in the West. Grammar-translation method had a natural evolution and teachers found it a very convenient method of teaching a language.

If religion was behind the emphasis on reading and writing, philosophy provided the rationale behind teaching the formal grammatical rules of the language. The scholastic philosophy of the middle ages laid the solid foundation for the understanding of grammar as a universal phenomenon, or as we may call it today, 'the Universal grammar'. Man is endowed with a mind which obtains, retains, and recalls knowledge. Concepts are the material on which the mind functions and through which man learns and retains knowledge. Concepts are universal which the mind obtains initially by means of its contact with the reality outside through the senses. These concepts are the same for all men; the meanings of all languages consist of concepts which are the same for all men. The universal meanings are the content part of language which is expressed by means of varying symbols of the spoken and the written language. Therefore the logical conclusion is that all human languages are the same in the content an they differ only in the external expression. The underlying grammar, the rules for the organization of the words, phrases and sentences must, then, be the same for all languages. Based on such an assumption as this the grammars, of Greek and Latin came to be 'the Grammar' for any language. The scholars of the middle ages or of the early modern period seldom thought of the possibility for every language having somehow a unique grammatical structure. All that preoccupied the grammarian's mind was that language as such has a set number of categories and relations which though derived from the classical languages, were thought to be true for all human languages. Based on this assumption the grammar of the classical languages became the model for later grammatical prescription so characteristic of traditional grammars. In the L_2 classroom rules of grammar are formally taught and are explained. The formal explanations and memorizing the rules were meant to acquaint the learner with the language.

Grammar-translation method doesnot pay attention to the skills of the language. No functional techniques are used in the teaching of grammar, the principal appeal is to the intellect of the child rather than to the language faculties. In other words, language is taught as an intellectual discipline. Teaching Latin and Greek was thought of during the middle ages as a way of disciplining the mind just as mathematics was considered to be. As the chief targets were reading and writing, the communication aspects of language did not received any attention. The attitude to language fully governed the approach to teaching the language in the classroom. All teaching was an intellectual exercise and language in the context of grammar-translation method received the same treatment. The same intellectual and formal approach continues even today wherever grammar-translation method is employed of course, with several modifications. As this method focuses its attention on *reading* and *writing*, it is the method widely used even in present-day practices in the teaching of the classical languages like Greek or Sanskrit, with several advantages. But when it comes to the teaching of a modern language for purposes of communication, as an L_2, grammar-translation method poses several problems which will be dealt with later. Owing to its natural evolution and tremendous convenience, grammar-translation method survived the test of centuries as 'the Method'.

2. The Role of Grammar and Translation

With the kind of presupposition we have discussed in the preceding sections, the grammar-translation method concentrates on the teaching of formal grammar and translation. The traditional grammar did not make a distinction between *lexis* and *grammar*. Traditional grammatical definitions include those of nouns, verbs, adjectives and adverbs. Any grammar book would include features which defined, described and exemplified the categories above. Traditional grammar has always been accused of assuming a semantic approach to grammatical description than a pure syntactic approach. The categories of noun, verb, adjective and adverb etc. designate characteristics of meanings rather than symtactic functions. On the other hand there are symtactic categories of subject, object and verb which are mixed with the above categories and seldom are distinctions made in this regard.

Since all language was somehow considered grammar, there was nothing in traditional grammar which did not fall under the scope of grammar. Whatever today is the prerogative of the lexicographer were part of the traditional grammatical description. In other words, it could be said that the whole of traditional grammar on which grammar-translation method was based, was an analysis and description of words. Therefore today we say that theirs was a word-oriented grammar. The real significance of syntax and the organizational mysteries of English syntax eluded the grasp of traditional grammarians. But even though they centred their attention on the formal features and formal structure of words in terms of inflections and derivations as well as suffixations and prefixations, word order as a predominant feature and as the most sensitive spot of English language was discovered by traditional grammarians. Traditional grammars, thus, include considerable treatment of word-order in English.

Again, against this background grammar-translation method advocated the formal teaching of grammar, if the grammar of a language means all this, what the teacher should do is to make the pupils thoroughly familiar with the intricacies of such a grammar. If the study of Latin and Greek required the mastery over the bulk of conjugations and declensions, as well as the manifold rules and exceptions to the rules of grammar, then learning English grammar would require no less mastery of the formal features of grammar. All these were bound to happen as the grammarian's attention never happened to focus on the spoken form of language. Language skills, therefore meant nothing; learning English meant chiefly learning its formal grammatical features. The definition of noun as 'the name of a person, place or thing or as 'a naming word' was more important as a classroom teaching device than the use by the students of a noun in actual sentences. Again, we may emphasise that language for grammar-translation method was much more an intellectual discipline than a *living system* for concrete use by the pupils.

As a result, the teacher took resort to the formal explanations of grammatical points and expected the pupils to memorize the rules of English grammar, the definitions as well as the exceptions to the rules. The cumbersome memorization was intended to train the pupil's mind as the learning of arithmetic would do, there was no training of the language faculties resulting in the mastery of the language skills. The principal activity that went along with the learning of grammar, as we have seen, was translation. Translation was used in grammar-translation method with various purposes in mind. Translation from and to the L_2 was expected to result in the learning of language elements by means of a natural comparison with the language elements of L_1. By language elements is meant here the parts of speech as employed in the written language, the varied kinds of sentences had clauses (the main preoccupation in the study of English grammar), and the vocabulary (without a basic distinction between the structural items and the lexicon of the language).

Although translation achieved several purposes (we shall discuss them at the end of the present chapter), it was a poor device to teach the language as a living system. Translation and the formal learning of grammar proved effective in the learning of what we today call the classical languages, which except in academic and scholarly circles no one ever makes use of in normal course of life. The inordinate burden which these devices put on the pupils proved useless in the acquisition of a modern language like English which is taught for purposes of day-to-day communication and to be employed in life situations. Both formal learning of the grammar of English as well as translation were carried out in fact in writing with the result that language learning in grammar-translation method became one of learning the written form of the language.

3. Stress on Written Language

Traditional grammar laid excessive stress on written language for reasons that have already been examined. Unlike present-day grammars which venture grammatical descriptions of the spoken language of contemporary period with its spatio-temporal constrictions, with illustrations exclusively from the relevant usage of the day, traditional grammar contain analysis of classical works with grammatical illustrations only from classical writers. Even Otto Jespersen who was a professed pioneer of the structural description of spoken language, in fact, uses illustrations chiefly from English classics. Jespersen's seven volumes of 'Modern English Grammar' (1909 to 1949) and the 'Philosophy of Grammar" (1924) are instances of the continued attachment of even modern scholarly grammarians to the written from of language.

Following the assumptions of traditional grammar in regard to the status of written classics of the language, grammar-translation method employed techniques for working on written material in the foreign language teaching classroom and to develop reading and writing. It is certainly not that reading as such received any explicit attention as a language skill, but as a component complementary to writing, reading, also received attention. Of the several techniques employed in the teaching of written language, translation was the predominant of all. Other techniques were : explanation of the content, analysis of sentences and clauses into component grammatical units, written question-answers, precise writing, and dictation. The teacher in the classroom dealt with a lesson in the textbook in the following ways:(1) *explanation* of the content material of the lesson in a progressive and phased manner, (2) sentence and clause analysis, (3) giving the L_1 equivalent of difficult words and purposes of illustration of meaning. (4) The pupils *read* the lessons aloud and answered questions in writing. The whole method consisted of a movement from explanation and analysis to writing answers to questions. *Dictation* formed a very important part of language teaching. The pupils learned the spellings of words and their meanings at home. The spellings, in turn, were reproduced by the pupils during dictation. Reading aloud and dictation were the only occasions when the pupils could get acquainted with spoken language, the spoken equivalent of what the children constantly put in writing.

Language learning in grammar-translation method was a progressive movement from written forms to spoken forms. The letters of the English alphabet, for instance, formed the basis of learning English words. The sound came secondary to and dependent on spellings. Pupils learned the spellings much before they picked up the spoken forms or the actual pronunciations of words. The pronunciations of a words such as *cut* and *put* were dependent on the way they learned the words: 'c-u-t' and 'p-u-t'. While confronting or trying to remember the words again what came foremost in the child's mind was not the sound-images of the spoken forms 'put or cut' but the visual images of the spellings. The L_2 learner of English thus depended on *spellings* for their *pronunciation*: some things quite contrary to the natural way the native child learned English. A Major reason for the failure of *Indian learners of English* in mastering correct pronunciation is in fact this dependence on the visual images of English spellings which are paradoxically different from and at times opposed to the correct pronunciation of contemporary period. This was a conspicuous outcome of an exclusive concentration on written language.

4. Drawbacks of Grammar-Translation Method

As grammar-translation method as a foreign language teaching method is tagged on to traditional grammar and medieval philosophy, an assessment of the method can be made only in the light of traditional grammar. The drawbacks of traditional grammar naturally become part of the method too, and as a foreign language teaching method a such grammar-translation method has its own characteristic deficiencies. First of all the very assumptions on which the method is based are wrong. Written language cannot be the sole basis of language study and language analysis, for reasons which we saw while discussing the priority of speech over writing. Spoken language is the living, dynamic and evolving language and its written forms solely cannot be representative of the language of a given period. Therefore the emphasis of writing in grammar-translation method is without foundation. The textbooks prepared under grammar-translation method contained extracts as well as abridgments of classics. The classics of English do not in any way represent either the present-day spoken language or even the written language of today. It sounds sheer nonsense that the learner of a modern language shall be introduced before anything else to the classical writings of the language which are infact meant for those already advanced in the study of the language.

Reading and writing in the classical language as well as formal explanations of grammar do not lead to the mastery of the skills of the language. A large part of the class period consisted in the use of the L_1 for purposes of L_2 comprehension. This again was a baseless practice. Intense work done in L_1 can never lead to practice in L_2 unless L_2 atmosphere itself if created in the classroom. Those who taught English through grammar-translation method largely did not handle English the way needed as there are enough loopholes to the use of English in the classroom under the shade of the method. Present-day *bilingual method* advocates a thoroughly systematic and judicious use of L_1 as a teaching aid; grammar-translation method, on the otherhand employed the mother-tongue not as a carefully-to be-used teaching-aid but for purposes of large-scale translation and explanation in which L_1 mostly took the place of L_2 in the classroom. A classroom where the pupils listen to and speak Hindi will end up in obtaining more practice in the skills of Hindi than picking up English.

In spite of advocating all sorts of teaching techniques and modern methods of teaching English in India, the rural schools as well as those urban schools where L_1 is the medium of instruction grammar-translation method is deep-rooted. Teachers with reasonable language proficiency are attracted to and appointed in English medium schools. Consequently those whom schools with the L_1 medium get are those who possess only the nominal qualifications. Again there is another side to the whole story; the absence of *English atmosphere* curtails the morale of even those who are resourceful and creative. Teachers who would like to employ new teaching methods in which they are trained and have the ability to do so are demoralised and discouraged as they find for themselves that they are expected to work on the one hand with a set of colleagues who have professed themselves in the use of L_1 only, and on the other with a group of students who have no language background in the *classroom*, in the *school* or at *home*. These isolated teachers with language proficiency and good will too end up in the use of L_1 only in the classroom as this ultimately becomes an existential question to maintain any sort liaison with the students and with the rest of the staff. This is a basic reason for the survival of grammar-translation method as the only method especially in rural India. In such circumstances the English classes do not have the advantages of a thorough 'grammar-translation class' for various reasons. The Government provides the teacher with structural syllabus and a textbook prepared on structural principles, but present-day English learners in rural India do not have either the pleasure of reading and working on a good lesson which in actual grammar-translation method would have been extracts from good classics, nor have they the pleasure of listening to good *spoken English* as is expected today on the basis of the structural textbook. Consequently the present-day L_2 learner of English in India is devoid of the advantages of both, the grammar-translation method and structural approach.

Again, grammar-translation method makes use of *translation* from the very early stage of the learning of L_2. Translation has place in fact at all levels of languages learning *i.e.* right from the primary stage to college level. Translation can be as simple as it can be the most complex exercise. But translation for grammar-translation method, as we have seen, was not a mere technique; it was the whole and sole of teaching the textual lesson. Carried to this extreme, translation becomes futile and burdensome for the child who is expected to function almost like a translation machine. A living language such as English when taught as an L_2 is required undoubtedly to get established in the mind of the child first of all as a *spoken language*, not as a system of writing. In the learning of English what the learner primarily needs is proper *English* atmosphere through which alone will the linguistic internalization take place. Translation if and when used should be build on the minimum base of spoken language.

In a classroom where grammar-translation method is used, the pupils are more heavily burdened than the teacher. Grammar-translation method requires a more resourceful set of learners, than a resourceful teacher because the role the teacher is expected to play does not require so much inventiveness and resourcefulness a would be required under the direct method. Committing things to memory is a chief component of grammar-translation method. Language learning is not a process of memorizing although some level of 'memorization' is involved. The native child learning L_1 does not voluntarily and all at once commit things to memory, instead he picks up the language through continuous and unbroken familiarity with the elements of the language. The skills of a human language, and its structural patterns are not meant for memorizing but to be mastered in course of time by means of practice and consequent formation of habits which are component elements of the language skills. In short what grammar-translation method missed most was the precious foundation of language skills.

5. Merits of Grammar-translation Method

Grammar-translation method with all the drawbacks discussed above, is not without significant advantages of its own. It has often been noted that people trained under the grammar-translation system has perfect mastery of *written English*, the spellings of English words and the formal grammar of English. How far this is true way it is said, we do not know. No research is known to have gone into the efficacy of grammar-translation method, but one thing is certain that a concentrated effort to teach and learn written English as in grammar-translation method has borne fruits in the area of writing. People who were trained under the grammar-translation method are known for their flawless writing, good handwriting, good spellings and good knowledge of the details of English grammar, things which our present generation deplorably lack. The author has had the experience of having learned Latin for a number of years through a pure form of grammar-translation method. Tremendous effort is made to learn the rules of grammar, the applications of the rules in writings, and to learn the correct forms of words. Although it means a lot of memorizing, the fruits in regard to the mastery over the written language are great. Today with our fresh emphasis on the spoken form of language, it is indeed a pity that the pupils pick up neither spoken English, nor good writing. Spellings for the present-day generation are a real stumbling block. But the author, as is ready to confess, would recommend good speech and good pronunciation even it if means the loss of mastery over spellings. Most of the English spellings are the remnants of the Old and Middle English forms, and our pupils cannot be encouraged to sacrifice spoken language and present-day English pronunciation for these antiquated spellings. Yet the mastery over the aspects can be considered an advantage of the emphasis on written language in grammar-translation method.

Another conspicuous advantage of the grammar-translation method is in favour of the teacher. The grammar-translation method does not expect the teacher to be highly resourceful. Any average teacher can teach through the grammar-translation method. Explanation of grammatical points are made in L_1 which any teacher will be able to do. The students translate material from and into the L_2; the teacher need only to supervise the work of translation. *Dictation* forms part of almost every class, which creates no problem for the teacher. The teacher is not expected to be in anyway active in class as for purposes of 'illustration, dramatization, demonstration or for introducing any other technique. There is mostly *writing* in class during which the teacher is relatively free. It is chiefly due to reasons such as these that grammar-translation method unofficially continues to be the only method of teaching mainly in the rural parts of India.

Grammar-translation method continues to be the asylum of inexpert, unresourceful, and incompetent teachers on the one hand, and of disillusioned and demoralized teachers, on the other, who due to several reasons are not prone to exert their creative intelligence and imagination in making classroom teaching a rewarding experience. In all such instances all that the teacher is willing to do is to be merely present in the classroom and keep the pupils somehow busy. In present circumstances when the English teacher is introduced into manifold techniques of active classroom teaching, only those teachers mentioned above can conveniently seek resort in teaching a modern language like English through grammar-translation method. The resourceful teacher will naturally move out of the aura of such a method and enjoy teaching as an *active*, *creative* and rewarding experience.

5
Structural Approach

1. The Basic Principles

Pragmatism in philosophy, *behaviourism* in psychology and *structuralism* in linguistics were the early twentieth century trio which exerted great influence on the teaching of foreign languages between the World Wars. Structural approach developed as the result of extensive researches held in the area of language teaching by those structuralist linguists who were predominantly interested in foreign language teaching methods. All the characteristics assumptions of structuralism in linguistics one way or another helped evolve an approach to language teaching, which is an antithesis on the one hand to traditional understanding of grammar as well as to grammar-translation method. The contrastive assumptions in both traditional grammar and structuralism have been examine in the foregoing sections. The following assumptions of *structural approach* are fundamental: (1) Language as reality is structured and the structure may be predicted and expressed as a set of elements holding a fixed set of relationships (Ch. 6, Sec. 4). (2) The functional views of language as *a process* and the analytic investigations carried out on language from such a perspective cannot lead the study of language any far. (3) Language is primarily *speech*; the speech habits of the community rather than writing alone can yield insights into the structure of language (4) The grammarian who sets out to study the structure of a language is expected to *observe* and *describe* the structural elements and organizational features of the language used by the community at a given period rather than prescribe rules in regard to the correct use of the language. (5) Correctness lies not on the pages of grammar books which tend to be considerably behind the evolving usage of the community, but it lies in the usage of the educated majority who carry out the affairs of a community.

Structural approach was evolved out of the basic propositions of structural linguistics, and the following basic principles characterise structural approach to the teaching of a foreign language: (1) Since language is essentially speech, priority and attention are given to speech in teaching a foreign language. (2) Language is essentially a set system of structures the mastery of which forms the core of language learning process. (3) The structures possess the characteristic of a logical sequence, consequently in the teaching of a language the structures are required to be thoroughly graded. (4) A fully graded presentation of the structures both in the textbook and in the classroom is a basic requirement in structural approach. (5) It is possible for the linguist to separate from all the language material what forms the *grammatical structures* of the language. In other words, English language has two fundamental sets of words: *structural* words and *content words*. (See for details Ch. 13) The content words get organized into sentence patterns by means of structural words. (6) Learning English consists therefore primarily in the learning of structural words and sentence patterns alongwith the required vocabulary. As for structuralism, *i.e.* in structural approach *grammar* consists of the structural words and sentence patterns, and the content words of the language form the *lexicon*. Accordingly, a sentence : *The merchant has been driving away all the beggars*, consists of three things in a structural approach analysis: (1) Structure words, (the, has, been, away, all), content words (merchant, drive(ing) and begger(s)), and sentence patterns (Active Voice, Present Perfect Continuous Tense, Simple Sentence etc.). (7) Practice in the use of the structures of the language alone will enable the learner to obtain mastery of the structures. (8) Lastly, a modern language such as English can be acquired only by means of a functional *i.e.* skill-oriented learning of the structures.

Structural approach, thus, provided an altogether new orientation to the teaching of English as a foreign language. The view that all elements that go into the structure of a sentence (Nouns, Verbs, Adjectives, Adverbs, Articles, Prepositions, Conjunctions etc.) are parts of the grammarians' task and all such elements must go as part of the teaching grammar does not find favour in structural approach. The study of *grammar* and that of *Lexis* (Vocabulary) are clearly distinguished in structural approach; classroom teaching should distinguish between the treatment of the structures and that of vocabulary. In grammar-translation method there is no systematic distinction between such component aspects of language as structures and vocabulary. Nouns, Verbs and adjectives are defined, examples and exceptions stated and categorizations are made: all as part of English grammar. Structural approach above all came out with a very scientific and systematic set of distinctions among the various aspects of teaching English as a foreign language: formal and functional language teaching, teaching of spoken language and writing, teaching of structures and vocabulary, of graded and upgraded material. It distinguishes between aspects of *presentation*, *practice* and *evaluation*; and more than anything else, the emphasis on the basic language skills as the essence of functional teaching is foremost in structural approach.

2. Maximum Use of the Foreign Language

The emphasis by structural approach on the teaching of the graded structures of a language means that the classroom should have the maximum foreign language environment. This is characteristic feature in structural approach. Where grammar-translation method is used the classroom is characterised by two factors :(1) practice in *reading* and *writing* and (2) maximum use of the *mother-tongue*. In reaction to these practices structural approach advocates methods which would include (1) practice in the speech-skills, not because reading and writing should be neglected (as would be the case in the direct method), but that the teaching of the graded structures can be better undertaken through aural-oral work.

This is something one may keep in mind in regard to structural approach. While discussing the *new structural approach* we shall examine more in detail its attitude towards the language skills. Structural approach entertains no prejudices against the teaching of reading and writing in favour of the aural-oral skills. This depend on the kind of specific method we attach to the principles of structural approach. But if at all there is any concentration on and advocacy of the use of the aural-oral skills in structural approach, it is due to the fact that the structural items and sentence patterns of English language along with the required vocabulary can best be taught through the aural-oral skills, and a functional learning of English language is possible only in terms of the aural-oral skills.

Thus without an active prejudice for reading and writing, structural approach advocates the use of the aural-oral skills in the teaching of the graded structures of English, by means of which English as a living language will be mastered by the L_2 learners. By and large the objects of structural approach can be achieved only if the classroom has the maximum possible English atmosphere. It means that the L_2 learners are exposed to the language of the teacher and of one another, which forms the sort of basis for the learning of the structures. Eventhough the classroom provides such varied use of the structures, on the one hand by the teacher himself, and on the other by the pupils, the language of the teacher alone is the target or what may be called and 'bull's eye' which the learner should aim at. The need for exposing the L_2 learner to different levels of language atmosphere and the way the internalization of the L_2 takes place are discussed under the chapter on Communication Skills. The entire programme of structural approach for the teaching of English as a foreign language by means of the presentation, practice and evaluation of the graded structures of English will reach no where unless due emphasis is placed on the aural-oral use of the language. Eventhough structuralism looks at language primarily and principally as speech, and structural approach to the teaching of English as a foreign language views English language principally as a set system of basic *structures* which should be thoroughly graded for purposes of teaching, the aural-oral skills *i.e.* listening-speaking skills logically come down to be the only effective means for attaining the required mastery of the basic English structures. What has happened in most countries where structural approach is employed for the teaching of English, is that *structural approach* as a set of basic teaching guide-lines have been procedurally implemented through methods like the direct method which entertain certain prejudices against the teaching of skills other than the aural-oral skills. Structural approach as such is not essentially attached to any one method, and the advantages of structural approach stand out only when a method proper to the linguistic background of the country goes with structural approach.

3. Gradation of Language Material

Structural approach upholds the teaching of English as a foreign language through the teaching of the structures of the language. The two factors related to the teaching of structures as we have examined and determining the effectiveness of the teaching of the structures of the language are : (1) an *aural-oral teaching* of the structures of English, and (2) *gradation* of the structures to be taught in class. The following can be considered some of the earliest structural items which the learner need to master: The basic tenses of English, the use of 'to be', 'to have' and 'to do' forms, the articles of English, the prepositions and the conjunctions. The questions which structural approach attempts to answer primarily are: (1) should the structural items and sentence patterns such as given above be graded ? (2) How shall they be graded ? and (3) what should be the fundamental principles of grading the structural items ? In trying to answer these questions related to the gradation of structures, we note that all the items mentioned above have the following features: The structures given above (for instance) are all not of the same priority; some of the structures seem more difficult for the learner to grasp and pick up than others. For example, *There is a book on the table* seem obviously much less difficult than *the boy is walking in the room* and this in turn is less difficult than *The girl has gone out of the classroom*. These structures, therefore should be placed before the learner at different *stages of sequence*. Secondly, the structures mentioned above do not have the same relatedness to each other. Every structure reveals some kind of logical relation to other structures. Unless structures revealing such a logical relatedness one put together and taught proximately, the learning of the structures cannot be functionally fruitful. It means that *The boy is walking in the room* and *A bird was sitting on the tree* are grammatically more related than the structures *The boy is walking in the room* and *A woman had sat on the bench*. Every structure some how proceeds from and is related to some other structure and an arrangement of the structures for teaching purposes on the basis of this relatedness is a fundamental requirement in structural approach. Lastly, the sequence of the structures need be established on the basis of what may be called, situational proximity, structural items and patterns which can be easily demonstrated in the classroom in all its concreteness without reference to situations which lie outside should be taught earlier than the rest of the structures. This situational proximity helps learners associate the structures with very concrete and life situations in a meaningfully related manner and obtain mastery over their use. For reasons such as these structural approach advocates a relatively thorough grading of the structures of the foreign language to be taught with a view of obtaining maximum results.

Again, what manner of gradation be followed? Should it be that the structures of English be neatly and sequentially graded once for all and begin teaching from one end of the list to another? This will be simply overlooking the seriousness of the problem of gradation. There are several factors which influence and determine the effectiveness of gradation. There are the various levels of students for whom the material is graded; *individual* differences affect the achievement of the pupils within any one level. The factors of *intelligence* and *memory* exert influence on the learning of the graded material. Language learning in the classroom, again, is not an unbroken and continuous process, unlike the L_1 learning at home. There are serious interruptions and time gaps which make the learning of the material difficult. For these reasons one of the fundamental principles correlated to gradation is repetition. Therefore a neat and sequential gradation of structures from beginning to end will not work. The learner requires time for internalizing the structure; internalization can takeplace only by getting exposed to the structure over and again. It means that the structures which occur earlier should not be neglected, but have to be formed part of the later material. This renders gradation difficult. The difficult ones and those that are problematic to the learner should meet satisfactory repetition. It is not only that repetition is enough if it is done in course of the entire English course in School. Every class *i.e.* every level will have a course in which the structures should find enough repetition.

Every time a new structure is presented in the textbook or in class, it has to be done on the solid basis of the previous, related structure. The adverb, the adverb phrases and the adverb clauses are grammatically related. It will be quite unwise of the teacher to repeat the adjective clause for presenting the adverb clause of reason. The adverb clause of reason *e.g. He has gone to the neighbour because the wants to get a book.* Should be introduced on the basis of a related structure like an adverb phrase of reason *e.g. He has gone to the neighbour to get a book.* A related structure is not any structure that happen to occur right before the new structure in the textbook. A related structure is one that has an immediate grammatical and logical relation to the new structure. Such an ordering of the material will result in better and quicker learning. Repetition of structures within a well graded structural system is very fundamental to structural approach.

Based on the above principles, a structurally graded syllabus will have *There is, There are* before *He has* and *They have*; and The present progressive tense (*The boy is walking in the room*) earlier than any other tense-patterns. In a thoroughly graded structural syllabus the pattern of simple present tense will come at a fairly advanced stage because the simple present is a complex notion (an abstraction) for the young learner to recognize. Structural gradation and presentation of the graded structures in terms of aural-oral skills make structural approach unique in several ways which we have discussed. The teaching of English as a foreign language, in tune with the manner of L_1 acquisition demands that a very natural sequence between various structures of English should be established just as the L_1 learner internalizes structural aspects which are easier, useful, proximate, concrete and particular earlier than their counterparts.

4. The New Structural Approach

It is necessary at this point to make a distinction between the basic form of Structural approach as attached essentially to Structural linguistics and behaviourist psychology and modified outgrowth *i.e.* the recent practices in structural approach as a result of recent investigations into the teaching of English as a foreign language. Such a shift into a modified form of strucutral approach has had several reasons : (1) The growing influence of cognitive field psychology is more or less doing away with the behaviouristic prejudices inherent in most present day investigations into language teaching; (2) the popularity recently gained by 'transformational generative grammar' in linguistics has further and substantially contributed to the understanding of language more from a 'mentalistic' view point contrary to the assumptions of the behaviouristic tenets. (3) Lastly, there has been a general awareness that endless rote repetition and programming in language learning have not brought foreign language teaching methods very far, and that some new thinking in this direction would be required to cope with the present day problems arising in the area of foreign language teaching.

The basic structural approach emphasized the teaching of graded structures rather than a haphazard reading and writing of classical pieces. The structures, further, are to be drilled by means of *aural-oral exercises*. The basic structural approach, as we have noted, places more emphasis on automatic drilling and mechanical manipulation of patterns with a view to establishing and consolidating the language habits. The entire work in the classroom is, thus, geared to an *automatic use* of the language by the learner without being aware of the patterns themselves in using language as it happens in the case of an L_1 speaker. The basic structural approach does not pay any significant attention to factors like the role of *meaningful practice* and the learning of the structures in meaningful and *life situations* which have become key-notes in the cognitive and transformational generative contexts. It may be stated that the paramount contribution of the new structural approach in the limelight of the principles of cognitivism and transformationalism is the new vistas which are opened up towards a *meaningful learning* of human language in life-like situations, having created the sort of language atmosphere in the classroom which is required for the proper internalization of the structures of the language.

The new structural approach has attempted to have a balanced attitude to all the four skills. With the structuralist background, structural approach initially placed considerable emphasis on the speech-skills after having associated with the direct method. The direct method which places exclusive emphasis on speech even at the expense of reading and writing, exerted great influences on the working of structural approach especially during the post-war periods. Especially in India the association of structural approach with the direct method in the teaching of English has caused considerable problems and misconceptions about the authenticity and effectiveness of structural approach. The new structural approach has been attempting to remedy this. As the direct method (we shall discuss later the basic and the modified direct method) itself has come to be modified so as to accommodate skills other than the speech-skills, the new structural approach has come to place greater emphasis on reading and writing and place all the four skills on a relatively important footing.

5. Emphasis on Meaningful Practice

The keynote of the new structural approach is its emphasis of learning English in meaningful situations and practice of the structures in life like situations. It is important therefore to examine the significance of automatic (Mechanical) and meaningful (situational) employment of a structure. It has been discussed that language learning as well as language production have two fundamental characteristics: (1) Language function takesplace at the *habit level*; and (2) language is a *communicational* activity with a basic purposefulness of its own. These characteristics are so fundamental that excessive stress on either of them is bound to result in a defective notion of language. Language as a habit and language a rule-governed and purposeful activity are almost the two sides of the same coin although in course of history schools of philosophy, psychology and linguistics have stressed one or the other of the two aspects of human language.

As human language functions on a habit level without having the necessity for the speaker to be consciously aware of the actual performance itself, language, on the one hand should be raised to the habit level through continuous practice. At the same time human language is not a sheer mechanical process; the human mind requires to assimilate the meaning and purposefulness of linguistic performance. Just as language has to be raised to a habit level through practice, the child should experience language in meaningful situations and should be able to use it as a purposeful behaviour.

In the context of the new structural approach, due place is given for both these aspects of language learning. It recommends *mechanical practice* of the concerned structures in fully set and stereotyped patterns to that the learner will gain automatic mastery of the structure on the other hand strucutral approach recommend *meaningful practice* of the concerned structures in situations independent of any set visual patterns so that the learner will be in a position to employ the structure independently in actual living situations later. The practical implications and the techniques of mechanical and meaningful practice will be discussed later under the concerned sections. The emphasis of structural approach on meaningful practice has made the approach more acceptable to and in tune with the present day trends. The meaningful applications of a structure are provided after a thorough practice of the structure in set mechanical patterns. These patterns provided visually on the chalkboard of the classroom enable the learner to place the structure in a visual context and obtain aural-oral practice. The great necessity for mechanical practice or rather of automatic mastery of the language will be discussed much in detail later. The native speakers of a language are capable of transacting any business and employing their language for purposeful communication of any kind without having the necessity to organise the patterns and items of grammar on the one hand, and of pronunciation on the other because they possess perfect proficiency of the basic language. This is the ideal for the L_2 learner of English. Learning and use of the structures of English should be continued until the learner will be able to construct sentences in actual living situations outside the classroom conscious only of the context rather than the actual language he is using. In otherwords, the ultimate goal of language learning is the use of the patterns of the language meaningfully for purposes of communication and social interaction. Unless the teacher takes full care of the learner's use of the patterns and strucutral items as well as of the vocabulary in life situations language learning will not serve the purpose for which it is meant present-day structural approach places considerable emphasis on this aspect of language learning.

6. Structural Approach in India

The history of structural approach in India goes back to the last phase of the British rule. From then onwards structural approach became the basis of teaching English in different parts of the country. The thorough English atmosphere in Universities and schools had been significantly contributing to the success of structural approach in India under the British rule. South Africa can be regarded as an example parallel to the India of the British days when English was compulsorily used in educational institutions of all kinds. The post-independent India has witnessed a gradual but continuous decline in the use of English in Educational institutions and we have reached a stage when English has become merely a nominal feature as part of present-day education, and an object of political tug-of-war.

Both of South Africa where English education greatly flourished as an L_2 and in India where English atmosphere has been on the decline the direct method is considered to be the heart and sole of structural approach. This association, as felt by many, has had several implications of the teaching of English as an L_2 in India. As a result of continued doubts regarding the efficiency of the English teaching methods in contemporary India, the Government of India appointed a *study group* in 1964, which was expected to submit its report to the Education Commission. The report which was accordingly submitted in 1966, felt that structural approach was increasingly used in various parts of the country and that it should be encouraged at an official level. The study groups also felt that a nation-wide campaign should be planned in training teachers of English in structural approach. The study group report of 1966 thus, was fully in favour of the structural approach as prevalent in the country.

Having been not satisfied with the report of 1966, the Government of India appointed another study commission to enquire into English education in the country, which submitted its report in 1971. The commission felt that an answer to the question of English education lay in *experiments* with new techniques and methods. The commission was not in fact satisfied with the prevailing mode of structural approach in the country, and felt that an ecclectic approach could be the only solution to the problem of English teaching in a country like India where the standard of English is declining fast. The commission was not against the use of structural approach but it was concluded that the association of structural approach with direct method was not in line with the atmosphere and requirements of the country. It was recommended that structural approach should be dissociated from the direct method and instead bilingual method (Ch.7) be used for an effective utilization of the resources of the learner's mother-tongue. Structural approach associated with the direct method can function successfully only where the most resourceful set of teachers are available and where some level of English environment is present outside the classroom. In present-day situation this is far from the truth and the commission recommended the use of the mother-tongue with clearly defined limits, a feature which is characteristic to bilingual method.

The association of bilingual method with the new structural approach would mean several things : (1) attention to oral work for the first two or three years, (2) a judicious use of the learner's mother-tongue in the teaching of structures and vocabulary, (3) planning and preparation of well-graded material for teaching purposes, (4) more attention to the *reading-skills* and *writing*, (5) emphasis on intentional, meaningful practice of language items. The commission of 1971 recommended concentration on reading after a considerable number of years of oral work as the necessary foundation for reading and writing. The concentration on *reading* is with a view to equipping the Indian students to meet the future requirements in reading as English is expected to become, as many seriously note, a reading or library language in India.

Structural approach in its new form has already been accepted as the officially sanctioned approach to the teaching of English in India. The State Governments sanction and promulgate a structural syllabus and a text-book prepared on the basis of structural principles for the teaching of English in schools. Structural approach in its modified form, as associated with ecclectic methods is accepted to be the official and formal way of teaching English in the country. As part of structural approach practised in India plenty of *extensive reading* material too is recommended to be included in present-day textbooks with a view to increasing the learner's reading proficiency. Although as it has been pointed out, structural approach is the official policy of India, our class-room in reality resound with the unscrupulous sound of the mother-tongue not as recommended by bilingual method, but of a defiant grammar- translation method with the free use of the L_1 only. This is the foremost explanation we would offer in a situation such as the present when English teaching has received its death-knell in our classrooms, and a revival would suffer no compromises.

6
Audio-Lingual and Direct Methods

1. L_1 in the Teaching of L_2

Foreign language teaching methods can be distinguished chiefly on the basis of two factors: (1) the stress put on the language skills, and (2) the attitude towards, the role of the L_1 in teaching the L_2. In the grammar-translation method the *mother-tongue* of the learner plays a major role so to say that in the classroom the L_2 is almost substituted with the L_1. In fact it may be asserted that in the grammar translation method the L_2 is taught in the medium of the mother-tongue. No systematic effort forms part of the grammar-translation method to *delimit* the use of the mother-tongue in teaching the foreign language. Explanation of formal grammar, the meaning of the vocabulary, classroom instructions and explanation of the content material of the lesson in the textbook are done in the mother-tongue of the learner. All these aspects as well as the role the mother-tongue plays in a grammar-translation class were examined in the respective chapter (Ch.4). With the onset of structuralism which already began reading to the heavy dose of the mother-tongue in the grammar-translation class, and of the structural approach which insisted on the priority of the structural aspects of language over anything else, the role of the L_1 in foreign language learning came to be looked at with suspicion. All arguments in favour of the use of the L_1 began to dwindle and there came a stage soon after the second World War when the *communicative value* of language alone received attention in foreign language teaching. Consequently the pendulum of foreign language teaching moved from one extreme of wholesale use of the mother-tongue to another of fully avoiding the resources of the mother-tongue with a view to establishing a full-fledged *foreign language atmosphere* in the classroom.

If such was the change of attitude to the mother-tongue in the teaching of the L_2, a lot need to be said regarding the exclusive shift in stress. As a reaction to the excessive emphasis grammar-translation method put an writing an on the classical written language, later scholars exercised an excessive shift of stress on the spoken form of language and on the speech-skills. In this connection we have three confusing schools apparently diverging at least in term of their mode of approach to foreign language teaching. They are (1) direct method, (2) structural approach, and (3) audio-lingual method. At this context it is necessary to place the three conceptions in their own perspectives, to avoid confusion. In fact the direct method which should have been discussed immediately after the grammar-translation method, and which is the trend oldest of the three is treated at the end of all the three. The direct method was a nineteenth century move in reaction to grammar-translation method which was in full swing at the time. Though it was the earliest of the three, the theoretical foundations of the direct method and the basic principles as an approach were to be fully developed later by the structuralists of the early twentieth century in giving shape to *structural approach*.

At the same time structural approach focused its attention on the teaching of the structures of the language and is not in any way identical in attitudes with the direct method. An identical set of principles based on the aural-oral, communicative value of language and direct relation between language and experience came to be systematically developed in what we today call 'the audio-lingual method'. While the direct method was almost a remote 19th century predecessor to structural approach, audio-lingual method is an offspring of structuralism in which *communication* is held as the very essence of language. It is due to the fact that structural approach is the only fully developed theoretical basis for foreign language teaching and the seeds of the later movements are embedded therein that we have dealt with structural approach at first and the others later. Several attitudes of foreign language teaching methods are identical in all the three and much efforts is called for to avoid repetition, and at the same time maintain the integrity and distinctions of each of the three stand points. It is for the same reasons that the direct methods and audio-lingual method are dealt with in the same chapter.

If the direct method may be considered the procuror of structural approach in reaction to the traditional grammar and the grammar-translation method, audio-lingual method is the true offspring of structuralist concepts which stressed behavioural, habitual, skill oriented and communicational aspects of human language. While the grammar-translation method sees no differences between the teaching of Latin or Sanskrit and a modern language like English, and apply the role of the mother-tongue to both in equal terms, the later methods see a modern language as a *living* and *evolving thing* and not merely an abstract corpus of forms and expressions for disciplining the human mind.

2. Evolution of the Direct Method

The 19th century witnessed considerable enthusiasm in changing over to some kind of active classroom methods in the teaching of foreign languages like English. The advocates of such active classroom methods exerted great influence on foreign language teachers. This new insight into language teaching came in the wake of a fresh understanding on the nature of language as an *active*, *dynamic* and *structured* system. The evolution of the direct method was based on the simple but significantly transitional belief that a learner learns a language simply by listening to it and speaking it a great deal. This new understanding came as a result of intense observation on the way children learned their language, in a context when foreign language were taught in the classroom as an intellectual discipline. People felt that language should be taught as an oral system by means of oral work, and that language teaching should some how come closer to the natural way the native child picks up his language. The direct method is the formal name by which the work of the advocates of the *oral* and *natural* way of language teaching came to be known during the 19th century. The background for the evolution of the direct method can be seen in the shift in emphasis of the role of the L_1 which is discussed in the section preceding. The Direct Method essentially consists of learning a foreign language without the medium of the mother-tongue and by having a *direct association* between language and experience *i.e.* words and phrases with objects and actions (see Section.3). Just as the native learner picks up new language with environmental factors : things, events, persons and features of experience, the L_2 learner is expected to master the meaning and the use of a language item by directly relating it to the reality or thing itself.

Several new features characterized the onset of the direct method as a foreign language teaching method (1) While in grammar-translation method learning English began with *reading* and *writing*, in the direct method speech is considered the solid basis for all language work. Speech preceded reading, and the few early years of the learner is expected to have thorough practice in speech only. (2) *Translation* into the mother-tongue as a learning device is thrown out of the foreign language teaching classroom. Translation is a predominant feature in the grammar-translation method for all aspects of classroom work. The direct method has absolutely no recourse to translation whatever may be its functional value. The idea is not to bring the L_1 material in any way into the classroom so that the L_2 is learned directly and without any recourse to the L_1. (3) Teaching through the direct method provides no room for any kind of a formal explanation of grammar. Functional grammar teaching (Section 4) is at the core of the direct method. Grammar in tune with the later structuralist conception is the very structure of language which does not consist in a set of formal rules to be memorized by the learner. Grammar in the direct method is a dynamic system consisting of the structures of the foreign language, which the learner understand by means of direct association. With situational experience (objects, actions, verbal devices) and learns to use by means of practice. (4) Correct pronunciation is an important feature of the direct method. Since the foreign language becomes the medium of instruction in place of the mother-tongue, the features of pronunciation came to have importance. The study of phonetics had already developed during the latter half of 19th century, which came as a great help to foreign language teachers. The notational system of the *international phonetic* Alphabet came as a great help to foreign language teachers who started an English language teaching course with some introductory work on the phonetic notations. For the sake of developing correct pronunciation of English sounds and words, the initial few months were spent in teaching only the pronunciation through the *phonetic symbols*. The great advantage was the students mastered actual pronunciation without getting confused over the spelling pronunciation dichotomy of English language. The students were allowed to see and read English words only after the correct spoken form of the words learned. By the time the complex and confusing written forms of the language were introduced, the students had already picked up the correct way of reading the words.

(5) From the beginning the learner listens to complete, meaningful sentences of the language by means of several *techniques*. As the teaching of the language items is in a functional way, just as in the case of the L_1 exposed to the full use of the language in relation to the para-linguistic contexts given shape in the classroom. They listen to the teacher's sentences in terms of verbal illustration, and questions which they answer in full sentences. Whenever possible in full-fledged discourse is provided as the background against which oral work could be held.

The outstanding characteristic of the direct method is whether in speech, reading or in writing, the classroom continually resounds with the foreign language and provides the necessary language atmosphere which, we are today convinced, is the chief requisite for language learning. The direct method follows again, the inductive way of enabling the listener to pick up the rules of sentence construction. The contracts with the language, and thorough practice in a variety of contexts help the learner gradually to derive for himself the regularity of the patterns of the language. By the time the students are required to learn the formal grammar of the language, the functional foundation is already laid in the sense that unlike in the grammar-translation method the students acquire the actual use of the structural aspects of the language and on its basis later learn the language as a formal intellectual system which consists of many abstractions. It is only in the formal teaching of grammar that the direct method employs *formal terminology.*

3. Direct Relation of Language and Experience

It has been said that the fundamental dictum of the direct method is its stand in regard to the relation between language and what we may call for convenience, experience. The grammar-translation method never seeks to bring home the meaning of linguistic units in terms of direct experience or contextual application instead the mother-tongue of the child is invariably and unscrupulously evoked at all circumstances to illustrate meaning, uses and explanations. This medium of the mother-tongue is what *direct method* attempts to avoid. The learning of a language is thought to be best done when it is learned all by its own, listening to it, speaking it and practicing it to the maximum possible extent, rather than getting it translated into the mother tongue for mere intellectual recognition.

Language has a very complex structure; as it has been noted, language presupposes a complex interplay of elements. The structure of speaking and listening, as well as all that goes into what we call communication have been the object of our discussion in *psycho-linguistics.* The two elements lying at the extreme ends of what we call language are: (1) *the sounds,* and (2) the reality of *human experience* or what we may call, the features, of human experience. Although in linguistic investigations we only speak of the sounds on the one hand, and *meanings* on the other, the term meaning is rediculously ambiguous unless specified for purposes of investigation. It is not proper to overlook the reality lying below what we call meanings *i.e.* what meanings represent. It is much more true when we consider such aspects for teaching purposes and try to understand the context in which language teaching-learning takesplace. For the young minds trying to pick up a new language the concrete aspects of classroom experiences are more significant and relevant than an abstract set of meanings which relates the two. Therefore in regard to the actual working of languages we may think of the two extreme ends: *the sounds* and the features of *human experience.* Every thing else in language is ordered between the two ends. Reality (the features of experience) is at once symbolized by what were called in earlier parts of this work as *conceptual elements;* these conceptual elements are in turn unified in a varied manner according to sociological specifications into *meanings*. Further the meanings are represented in words and expressions; when the words and expressions are phonologically specified as per language and are graphically represented we have writing, and as they are *phonated* we have the speech form of language.

What the direct method essentially does in the teaching of a foreign language is to relate the two: (1) the words and expressions (which consist of sounds) and (2) features of human experience, without bringing in the words and expressions of any other language. There are two reasons which the direct method holds dear in this regard: (1) the elements of a language can be learned only by using them in skill oriented practice, and (2) the meanings of different languages are structured differently by means of conceptual units, Therefore, first of all, translating words and expressions of another language *i.e.* the L_2 into L_1 is a deficient manner of introducing the meanings of the words and expressions as well as structures of the L_2, and, secondly translation causes the learner of the L_2, and, secondly translation causes the learner to listen to and speak in the L_1 rather than the L_2 thereby not meeting principle (1) mentioned above. It is for these reasons chiefly that the basic direct method does not make use of translation of any kind in foreign language teaching, eventhough this means added labour both on the part of the teacher and the pupils. Explanation of grammatical rules in the L_1 too are strictly avoided for the same reasons, as all explanations provide only intellectual recognition rather than development of the skill-oriented language habits.

4. Teaching Functional Grammar

The functional teaching of grammar forms another very essential part of the direct method. In present-day teaching of English in India there are quite a number of paradoxes found. The following categories of teachers are a common sight in the country: (1) teachers of English who have a fair command over the written language but have no speech proficiency whatsoever; (2) teachers who possess competent formal knowledge of the grammar of English language while they themselves are unable to produce fluent and correct sentences in speech; and (3) teachers who are trained in the latest methods and techniques of teaching English but possess no command whatsoever in the spoken or written forms of the language. These are to be considered paradoxical because in the absence of average proficiency of the language the counterparts mentioned are rendered useless What the English teacher requires is a command over the spoken language and everything else should begin from that. A scholar of English language is rendered a failure in the classroom if communication breaks down. What counts foremost is the teacher's *linguistic proficiency* in creating an English language atmosphere by means of his communicational involvement, whose language is the bull's eye for the pupils in the learning of English. The teacher's knowledge of the written language is rendered useless because of his inability to communicate the way the classroom requires; the teacher's knowledge of formal grammar bears no fruits as the target in the direct method is to train the pupils in functional grammar for which the teacher is not qualified. Lastly, the training in methods of teaching English counts for nothing as the teacher's organizational ability finds no outlet through proficient language.

As the direct method very rightly emphasizes, what the L_2 classroom basically requires is the functional teaching of English structures by a teacher who is fairly competent in organizing his classroom activities accordingly. The teaching of the formal aspects of English grammar such as the description and explanations of the grammatical units, their definitions and relations is aimed at for purposes of knowledge of the formal language. Whereas the teaching of the skills of the language and the practice provided in the skills are aimed at proficiency in the use of the language. In the contrasts we have drawn in three instances above, the latter is absent whereby the teacher is functionally, so to say, retarded. In a direct method classroom, an incompetent teacher of English is doomed to failure because of his inefficiency in providing functional practice of the structures and vocabulary in class. For reasons such as these a direct method class in the hands of an incompetent English teacher will be at once converted into a class in the grammar-translation method.

It is at a later stage *i.e.* towards the second half of a full-fledged English language course in the High school probably that we may introduce the formal aspects of English grammar, something which the pupils are bound to continue at the University level. But wherever the functional language teaching does not click and the pupils do not achieve proficiency in the language skills, the teaching of formal grammar is rendered useless and perhaps harmful at any level. One thing which any exponent of the direct method is most sure is that the learning of English as a foreign language can never be achieved by means of a formal learning of its grammar which functions solely as an abstract *quantum* of *knowledge*. English language learning calls for active, skill-oriented classroom practices where the English language atmosphere created by the English teacher serves as the functional basis for the pupils to *listen to*, *speak*, *read* and *write* English language. There is hardly any compromise in this regard.

5. Audio-Lingual Method

The post-war period with its recognition of the tremendous interdependence of the Nations of the world has been affecting an intense awareness of the need for thorough *international communication*. English is more and more recognized as a *world language* with all pre-twentieth century efforts to create an international language having failed. The present emphasis is consequently on the ability to communicate in the language of liaison rather than get to have deeper formal knowledge of the language as has been examined on the foregoing pages. The more the nations of the world interact on socio-economic and political levels, the greater has become the need to master the common language or what has been traditionally known as the 'lingua franca', the language of liaison. *Audio-lingual* is the term recommended by Nelson Brooks of Yale University to stand for the method of teaching a foreign language with a view to developing in the learners the aural-oral abilities to communicate through the language.

We have treated the direct method and audio-lingual method in the same chapter since they do not differ on the fundamental issues, and both the methods overlap considerably. It will not be presumptuous to remark that audio-lingual (aural-oral method) is a contemporary version of the direct method with a new emphasis on the *communicative value* of the foreign language taught in class.

The audio-lingual method aims at the following in a foreign language teaching classroom:

(1) teaching the foreign language as communication with a view to achieving development of communication skills. The new emphasis on being able to communicate in the foreign language has resulted in the systematic approach to the aural-oral skills in the classroom. The aural-oral method has emerged as the very foundation of the foreign language skills, on which to develop reading and writing. If structural approach is the application of the principles of structural linguistics to the teaching of languages and the emphasis on the teaching of the graded structures of the language, then audio-lingual method too originated. Within the fold of structural linguistics and behaviourist psychology with a set of trends parallel to structural approach but at the same time putting stress on the aural-oral, communicative aspects of language and the teaching of the same in the L_2 classroom.

(2) The scientific attitude which structural linguistics holds so dear is considered basic also to the audio-lingual method of teaching a foreign language. The second World War provided the background for the application of the principles of *scientific linguistics* (Structural Linguistics) to the teaching of foreign languages, originally in the United Stated of America. The United States Government called upon the structural linguistics as authorities on language to provide trained interpreters for purposes of liaison with the Allies. As a result selected personnel from the Armed Forces underwent a sort of training which was to remain for a long time to come a model for intensive language acquisition. It was a short term but very intensive training in the *aural-oral* skills of the foreign language concerned. A very high degree of aural-oral ability was the outcome of the intensive training provided for a few months. The secret behind the success of the training

lay in its strictly scientific and fully controlled set-up in which training was given in the aural-oral skills. This scientific attitude though followed less strictly in present-day practices is basic to the audio-lingual method.

(3) A high momentum of practice is the device by which in the audio-lingual method the in-taking of language takes place. Language is considered by the structuralists, a set of habits just as it is thought of as communication. Every language skill is the sum-total of a set of habits which the learner is expected to acquire. So far as practice is concerned, again, structural approach and audio-lingual method go hand in hand. As part of structural approach we discussed in detail the role of meaningful and mechanical practice (Ch.5 Sec.5). Both in the structural approach proper and in the audio-lingual method the present day practices include mechanical and meaningful practices as essential steps in teaching a structure or vocabulary. Practice as a whole, therefore is central to all the contemporary foreign language teaching methods, and with an added stress on it in the audio-lingual method.

(4) The stress put on the aural-oral skills at the early years of the foreign language course is continued during the later years and the aural-oral skills remains a centre of concentration throughout even when later reading and writing are introduced. The basic principle that the teacher is expected to follow especially when the audio-lingual method is followed along with structural approach is that the learners should *speak* only what have had a chance to listen to sufficiently; they should *read* only that material (structures, patterns and vocabulary) which they have used as part of their aural-oral practice; and they should *write* only that material which they have read. In other words strict sequential ordering of the material in terms of the four skills is recommended.

The audio-lingual method employs several useful teaching techniques whose details we shall look into in later chapters on teaching techniques. The main techniques employed for presentation of a new item are: demonstration, dramatization, (which fundamentally belong to the direct method) miming, verbal illustration or pictorial illustration. Mechanical practice is provided through techniques such as substitution tables pattern practice drills consisting of the structures, minimum vocabulary and the basic patterns concerned. Dialogues are provided visually for reading and practice of the structures used. To provide practice of the structures and vocabulary in meaningful situations question-answer series are employed. The questions are asked on independent classroom situations created para-linguistically by the teacher, or the questions are derived from some visual material such as a paragraph or dialogue or even picture on whose basis the pupils can answer questions. Practice of drills is usually in given individually as well as in groups. Practice is continued until the learners are able to manipulate the patterns on their own in independent life situations.

6. Merits and Drawbacks

There are many features common to structural approach, the direct method and the audio-lingual method that a closed description of any one of these is difficult. The distinctions of these approaches and methods may be drawn only in regard to their basic characteristics and against the background in which each took origin. In present-day classroom practices one will never find any one method exclusively used and it is good that it is so. The ecclectic methods used by teachers today subsume what is good and feasible in very method and make it colourful adding their own creative imagination. The quintessence of *structural approach* lies in strict grading of the structures of language and centering all language teaching around the structures; the quintessence of the *direct method* lies, on the other hand, in establishing a direct relation between language and features of human experience rather than bringing in the mother-tongue of the learner as the medium to obtain comprehension. The central concern of the audio-lingual method is training in the aural-oral skills of language and centering all language learning around the aural-oral skills. All other characteristics of language learning as have been the topic of our discussion in the forgoing sections are more or less common to all the three and these aspects cannot be distinguished as part of any one method or approach in present-day practices.

All the same it is possible to distinguish the *merits* and *drawbacks* of the audio-lingual method as relevant to the teaching of L_2 in our classrooms. Language in the structuralist context is an expression as well as the symbolic embodiment of the culture of a community, the teaching of a foreign language for purposes of communication simultaneously means an acquaintance with the culture of the community. Thus along with the introductions of the learners to a new language, audio-lingual method also rightly advocates the introduction of the cultural background of the language. In an era of intense search for international understanding and relations such as ours, it is befitting that foreign language learning should enable the learners to get introduced to the cultural life of another society, and know it intimately through the language. The greatest strength of the audio-lingual method is its concentrated effort to develop the communication skills with a view to enabling the foreign student to express himself as best as possible in the foreign language. The manifold techniques employed for this purpose do bear fruits in the hands of an efficient teacher.

The visual, audio-lingual and audio-visual aids recommended and developed by the pioneers of the audio-lingual method of language teaching have been to help in the classroom as well as in language laboratories and the method has brought the latest technology in to the area to foreign language teaching. The use of the *language laboratory, reading laboratory, radio, television, play-back machines, teaching machines* for programmed instructions, *video tapes, slide-projectors, over-head projectors* and *opaque projectors* mark the technological advancement of contemporary education as a whole and language teaching in particular. In the present-day educational space *satellites* we have the climax of all technological applications. The audio-lingual language teaching method has laid the foundations for the application for modern technology to the teaching of language.

Compared to a class in grammar-translation method, audio-lingual method provides great enthusiasm and motivation in the learning of foreign language. The concentration on listening and speaking keeps the learners happy and enthusiastic in learning the language. The introduction of the new material by means of activity oriented techniques and life situations bring L_2 teaching closer to the L_1 learning situations. Audio-lingual method meets several of the language learning requirements we mentioned in our treatment L_1 learning under *psycho-linguistics*. Audio-lingual method alone is capable of providing satisfactory *L_2 atmosphere* in the classroom which is pre-requisite for the internalization of a new language as demanded in the transformational generative system. Unlike the basic direct method, the audio-lingual method also provides due place for the development of reading and writing skills. A earlier phases the learner is provided with reading material on the basis of only what he has used in speech. At later, more advanced, levels more independent reading material is provided in the form of supplementary readers. The same is true of writing in which practice is given at earlier stages by means of thoroughly controlled and guided composition of very elementary type, and such as simple transcription and sentence-construction and moves towards more independent writing until the student can freely express himself on a topic in writing within broad outlines provided by the teacher.

There are quite a few weakness if either the direct method or the audio-lingual method are strictly applied in teaching practices. A strict adherence to aural-oral practice alone in the classroom during the early years of the pupil's school life is bound to set in some level of boredom. Reading and writing provide the kind of variety which pupils need in course of the day. There is, again, the problem of practice: a fully audio-lingual class would resemble to a laboratory for guiny-pigs. Although drills and repetitions practice to have their good place in language learning, an excessive stress on drills may adversely affect language learning. Language is best learned in *life*-like, *meaningful* and *creative situations* rather than through repetitive patterns practice. Appeal should be made to the pupil's creative resources than merely to the habit-forming faculties. Both in the basic direct method and in the audio-lingual method, the learner's mother-tongue is fully avoided. This has certain serious consequences as we shall be examining it in the following chapter. There are times when the

L_1 can be of tremendous help provided the L_1 is used within strict methodological guidelines. Lastly, the audio-lingual method, just as the direct method requires very resourceful and proficient teachers which most countries where English as an L_2 is taught pitiably lack. Structural approach, the direct method and the audio-lingual method in their own way contribute magnificently towards the teaching of English as a foreign language, but none of these methods is probably *the answer* to the large question of foreign language teaching. Foreign language teaching is a continually evolving factor, and answer are bound to be temporary as situations keep on changing.

7
Bilingual Method

1. The Background

The initiation of *Bilingual Method* into the teaching of foreign languages has opened up new vistas of knowledge and possibilities in regard to the use of the L_1 in foreign language teaching. The history of foreign language teaching methodology has almost always seen extreme approaches either in the form of grammar-translation method, the direct method or the reading method. While the grammar-translation method placed exclusive emphasis or writing and written language the direct method concentrated on speech and direct language-experience relationship, and the reading method of Michael West considered only reading as worthwhile among all the four skills. The extremities lay in two aspect: (1) emphasis of the *language skills* in the teaching of a foreign language, and (2) the role of the mother-tongue in the teaching of the foreign language. In the grammar-translation method, the L_1 is almost substituted in the classroom in the teaching of the L_2. The major role L_1 plays in the grammar-translation method is based on the assumption that the L_2 can be learned best by comparing and contrasting to the L_1 features. By aiming at such grammatical comparison as the outcome of the grammar-translation method, stress is put on the one hand, on all the four language skills and on the other, the learner's mother-tongue it restored to its due status as the L_2 learners most potential resource. The initiation of *bilingual method*, thus, is the answer to a far-reaching cry to restore the dignity and potentiality of the learner's mother-tongue which was totally ignored and neglected in the direct method and in the structural approach.

The origin of *bilingual method* goes back to Prof. Dodson of the North Wales University, who made use of Welsh in the teaching of English and other foreign languages with a view to discovering the efficacy of systematically an judiously using the L_1 in the teaching of an L_2. The assumption most fundamental to the Bilingual method of Prof. Dodson is that the mother tongue of the learner is the most potential resource at his disposal in the learning of a language, and instead of shutting the door upon the *mother-tongue*, the resource should be systematically employed in the teaching of the foreign language. Once this is done, the following advantages will be derived in a foreign language teaching classroom: (1) Much of the laboursome activities of the teacher in *introducing* a language item will be eliminated by systematically replacing the activities with the learner's mother-tongue. (2) The most complex and *activity-oriented* class in the direct method and the linguistically indirect comprehension procedure for the learners are simplified in bilingual method by means of judicious use of the mother tongue. In the grammar-translation method, the burden is on the pupils by way of translation, memorizing and written question-answering; by contrast in the direct method the burden is on the teacher by way of initiating classroom activities and introducing language items through situational factors. Bilingual method attempts to strike a medium in terms of distribution of work between the teacher and the pupils. (3) A class in the grammar-translation method did not call for much resourcefulness on the part of the teacher; a class in the direct method called for great initiativeness and resourcefulness on the part of the teacher. Between these two extremes an average teacher (as is mostly the case in present-day classrooms) can very well manage a class in bilingual method if he is conversant with the aspects of the method. (4) The sounds of the mother-tongue and the words with which the learner is intimately conversant provide a congenial atmosphere in a foreign language classroom; the very mention of an equivalent in the mother-tongue in an English class brightens up the young faces in contrast to the labour a helpless teacher undertakes to bring home the some idea through activities and illustrations in English.

Keeping aside the advantages of the bilingual method mentioned above, there are quite a few claims made by the method. The *Bilingual Method* claims to put equal stress on all the four skills unlike other methods of foreign language teaching. Different stages in course of a lesson are set of take care of every language skill. It also claims to strike a balance between *fluency* and *accuracy*. The grammar-translation method provides accuracy in whatever work it does such as the knowledge of formal grammar, ability and accuracy in written language, on the other-hand the direct method is said to provide fluency in spoken language at the cost of accuracy. Bilingual method is expected to aim at providing both fluency and accuracy in language learning, factors of which one cannot be scarified for the other. Yet another claim made in bilingual method is that it provides ample time for practice because the time usually taken up in a direct method class for presenting some material, is cut short to the minimum by the introduction of the mother-tongue. Bilingual method leaves enough scope for the growth of the child's imaginative and creative aptitudes by not spoon-feeding the child with everything. A systematic utilization of the mother-tongue is expected to achieve all these in bilingual method.

2. L_1 as Teaching Aid

The fundamental characteristic of bilingual method is its attitude towards the learner's mother-tongue. In it we find a legitimate revival of the nobility of the mother-tongue and its role in foreign language teaching. The long-neglected first language is brought to bear upon the learning of the L_2. The first language is the child's basic asset; for the child the first language is behaviour, communication, achievement, and fulfillment. The child cannot be thought of or defined as a growing and maturing personality apart from the first language he has acquired. It is almost identical with his personality unlike any other language he will learn in later years. The first language is intimately linked with the child's biological, psychological and social fulfilment. These were the purposes for which the language was acquired primarily. Unlike a foreign language which the child learns later, the development of the first language is linked directly to every phase of the child's *psycho-sociological* development.

It is such a *resource* as part of the child's built in personality that almost all foreign language teaching trends of the structuralist school have been keeping out of the classroom. In keeping out the first language we have deprived the L_2 learner of a large bulk of his dynamism and made him artificially silent when his very personality surges with enthusiasm to know and speak in a language which is all part of him. Yet we cannot go so far as the grammar-translation method in permitting the L_2 learner employ the L_1 with all the satisfaction that might be derived out of it. Bilingual method with all the *methodological precautions* permits the teacher bring the harnessed horse of the mother-tongue into the classroom with a view to utilizing this powerful resource in the teaching of the foreign language.

This would mean that the mother-tongue is used in the classroom not as the medium of teaching as happens in grammar-translation method, but as a teaching technique or if we are allowed to say, as a teaching aid. Once let loose the mother-tongue pervades the whole of classroom teaching; instead it is used only of well-defined steps of teaching and in clearly defined manner. In using the mother-tongue the teacher in the grammar-translation method has all the freedom of expressing himself in it, and the teacher in the direct method has no freedom at all in using the L_1; but bilingual method strikes the middle and permits judicious freedom in the use of the first language. The term judicious is very significant in bilingual method because once the legitimacy is overstepped, the teacher will easily transform his bilingual class into one in the grammar-translation method.

3. Integrated Teaching of the Skills

Bilingual method is expected to put stress on all the four skills on an equal footing. Grammar-translation method grossly neglected spoken language and all activities in the classroom were directed to the development of writing and written language. The direct method on the otherhand, is aimed at the development of the aural-oral skills of the foreign language, and the audio-lingual method, despite its professed attitude to the development of all the four skills, concentrates throughout more on the aural-oral skills of the foreign language. Bilingual method is aimed at overcoming whatever deficiency there is in regard to the partial emphasis on the language skills.

An integrated approach to the language skills in an important requirement to make foreign language teaching a success. The communication skill of speaking certainly calls for concentrated efforts on the part of the teacher; at the same time, reading and writing are aspects of language teaching which have great significance especially in our country taking into consideration the majority of the English learners in our country who infact employ English for *purposes of speech*. It is possible for us to contrast the classical languages against modern languages in the present context. The classical languages (*e.g.* Latin or Sanskrit) cannot possibly be revived as active, living languages for purposes of communication in society; all the same, the classical languages survive in their written forms and the learners of such languages are required to learn these language only for purposes of reading and writing, and not for speech. No ordinary purpose is served by taking pains to revive such languages in this *spoken forms*.

The same is not the case with a modern language such as English. Either speech, reading or writing cannot be neglected for any reasons whatsoever when English is taught as an L_2 in a country like India. Neglecting anyone of these skills is mutilating a modern language like English all aspects of which are so relevant to modern life that neglecting any one of the skills goes very much against the dynamism of the language. The one-sided and prejudiced attitude that educationist, theoreticians or teachers may develop in regard to the teaching of English will not be forgiven by the generations to come, who will have to face the consequences of such a negligence. The only feasible solution to the problems arising from the area of *teaching English* is an integrated approach to the skills of English. The following is meant by the integrated teaching of the skills of English:

(1) Adherence to the natural, psychological sequence of the four basic skills of English. It would mean that there can be no excuse whatsoever in putting the cart before the horse and teach reading and writing at the start. If English language teaching in the country has reached such pitiable stage as we have today, the reasons could be traced back to the great neglect of the basic principles of language teaching which have throughout our post-

Independence history of English teaching remained on the pages of books. It does not mean that for several initial years speech should be the exclusive object of practice. Instead, during the initial years the pupils should be put under competent hands who will provide them with a satisfactory foreign language atmosphere in which the pupils will get continually acquainted with the basic *structural* items *sentence patterns* and *vocabulary* of English through speech. It is not a process of memorizing words or patterns, but one of getting *acquainted with* and in course of time *internalizing* the language.

At the same time, as is required to avoid boredom, side by side the teacher will introduce the pupils to small doses of reading and writing of the material which have been made familiar to the pupils through speech. Whatever dose of reading and writing is introduced should be done only after an exclusive work with the basic spoken language at least for six months. This may cause little boredom; but the boredom will be rewarding in the long run. Filling in the pages of books with sets of symbols which the pupils cannot even properly read would hardly justify the cause of English language teaching. English teaching at any level should begin with proper oral work and then continue along with reading and writing which can constantly be referred back to the work done in class.

(2) *Integrated teaching* of the language skills would also mean that a regular *sequence* is maintained even in a single class period. This need to be worked out in regard to the kind of lesson, the level of the learners and the achievement background of the learners concerned. Whatever work is done orally can be the material for reading and the source for writing. It is not necessary for any one period at advanced levels especially to be dedicated fully for speech, reading or writing. An integration of the skills can be achieved by means of regular sequence of the skills in every class period. Speech should form the beginning of language work and writing should form the end of it. Wherever the sequence cannot be maintained in any one period, a number of class periods will form a *unit* in which speaking, reading and writing of some material can be organized.

(3) Integrated teaching of the basic skills, again, can be

achieved by means of the following organization of teaching activities. :

(i) *presentation* of the new language item,

(ii) *mechanical practice* of the item in set verbal contexts,

(iii) *meaningful practice* of the item in varied life situations,

(iv) *evaluation* of the item by means of some competent exercises,

(v) *oral-composition* on some relevant topic employing the language item in which the pupils construct *discourse*; and lastly

(vi) *written composition* of some topic using the language item, in which a discourse is developed in writing. In between the oral composition and the written composition the teacher can find some relevant material for purposes of *reading*.

A work of this kind on some language item can be stretched over to a period of two or three English classes if necessary. But an approach of this kind is bound to provide a unified language experience which will indeed to rewarding.

(4) Integrated teaching of the skills, again, means that the *textbook* used at the particular level may be considered the source from which all activities in the classroom could emanate; if the textbook is resourceful and well prepared it will become the centre of all language activities in the classroom. The textbook is a concrete source on which both the teacher and the pupils depend. The rest of the classroom activities should be organized as experiences emanating from the textbook. A resourceful teacher draws plenty of material on the basis of the textbook for speech, reading and writing. All sorts of language experiences will be unified in the classroom on the basis of the textbook provided it is placed in the hands of an effective teacher.

Bilingual method claims to give due place to the four skills of language. Prof. Dodson's recommendations in this regard are espoused in his book: 'Bilingual Method', in which Dodson specifies the steps where the mother-tongue should be employed for purposes of immediate recognition, where reading can be undertaken and where the pupils are required to write. The present work has taken into consideration only the spirit and the basic principles of bilingual method and no effort is made to include the details of classroom activities the techniques and the steps which are recommended as part of bilingual method. Teaching English in India by the author includes the details of all aspects of teaching English in the classroom; at the same time, in the last resort it is left to the English teacher functioning against a particular background to decide as to how a lesson should be organized to the very details in the light of what has been included in the present work. Every English teacher is required to be aware of the need for an integrated approach to the teaching of English, and the spirit of bilingual method provides enough scope for integrated language experiences in the classroom where all language skills are given equal attention.

4. Balance of Fluency and Accuracy

There is a certain claim, again, in bilingual method, of a balance between *fluency* and *accuracy*. In the grammar-translation system there is definite emphasis on accuracy. By accuracy we mean a concentration on learning things the most correct manner possible rather than learning a wide variety of language-features. The grammar-translation method aims at mastering the written forms of the language, the spellings of words, the grammatical and idiomatic expressions, and the formal rules of the language to the pupils' maximum capacity of correctness. It aims at clarity rather than variety correctness rather than speed, and accuracy rather than fluency. By contrast to these, the direct method as well as the audio-lingual method lay comparatively less stress on the accurate mastery of language items in terms of grammatical and idiomatic correctness than quicker mastery and fluent use of the language. The heavy dose of practice and repetition are meant to acquire a more speedy mastery and fluent use of the language.

Bilingual method claims to meet the requirements both for *fluency* and *accuracy*. In the last resort, again, it depends how well the teacher is to organise the classroom experiences which will lead to the development of language in such a way as to meet fluency and accuracy. Teaching English in contemporary times cannot afford to neglect either fluency or accuracy. But it depends what the teacher or the theoretician means by accuracy. If accuracy means correctness, it is a very ambiguous and vague concept today. What is correct and what is not correct in terms of the very details of usage cannot easily be determined. At the same time the pupils can be made conversant, at advanced levels, with various possibilities of expressing the same thing with the fundamental grammatical correctness, all of which are accepted uses.

While *fluency* can be thought of only in terms of speech, *accuracy* goes both with speech and writing. The grammar-translation method took care of accuracy in writing as adherence to the norms of basic grammar, idiomatic expressions, spellings and norms of graphics. Fluency, in the sense we understand it as a quality of speech has no place in the grammar-translation method. Fluency is essentially an aspect that goes with those methods which lay stress on speech. Along with *fluency* can be considered *accuracy* which in spoken English will consist in adherence to the norms of basic grammar, idiomatic expressions, pronunciation including the prosodic features such as stress and intonation, and aspects of detailed use of modern English. The teacher in the classroom, therefore, requires a close acquaintance with all the aspects of accuracy in language mentioned above. It is in short a close acquaintance with the way English is used both in *speech* and in *writing*.

With all the emphasis we lay on *communication* today, the pendulum is bound to swing on to fluency than accuracy, the present-day circumstances as they are. The stress what we lay on the spoken form of the foreign language should lead to a speedy as well as thorough acquisition of the foreign language. But at the same time, as bilingual method advocates, today we require a correct and rational approach to both speech and writing as noted in the section on 'Integrated approach to the skills'. At attempt to pick up acceptable form of spoken English may not lead to a neglect is learning acceptable written language. Whatever be the shift in problems that we face or the shift in policies, the integrity of a modern language like English calls for an *integrate approach* to the language terms of fluency and accuracy as well as of the basic skills of the language. The bilingual method by relating the L_1 to the teaching of L_2 as the principal aid, is aimed at saving considerable time and there by channeling the resources and using the time available for an integrated teaching of the language skills as well as for achieving fluency and accuracy in the use of the foreign language.

5. The Simplicity of Bilingual Method

Perhaps, the most attractive feature of bilingual method is its essential simplicity in terms of the teaching techniques. The grammar-translation method is too simple for the teacher at the risk of actual language learning; the direct method lays great burden on the teacher as the Method has complex organization of teaching techniques. But simplicity in teaching techniques is ever more recommended in present-day teaching practices. Simplicity of teaching method is required due to a variety of reasons: (1) no language teaching method can take as the norm the ideal teacher, as few ideal teachers are to be found in actual classrooms. The methodological recommendations made should be within the ability range of the average teacher as average teacher crowd the foreign language teaching scene. (2) Too complex language teaching methods will create learning problems, again, for the average and below average learner. The learner is to be kept in mind in developing foreign language teaching methods. Any method which makes the *learning process* complex cannot be recommended for the classroom. (3) Again, *simplicity* of method is required so that the method will be applicable in a variety of language teaching situations as well as against a variety of linguistic backgrounds.

Simplicity of teaching methods would consist of the following. A simple language teaching method avoids undue stress on any particular aspect of learning. Any such undue stress would result in gross neglect of several important aspects of learning. Method concentrating on speech would pay little or no attention on the development of the reading and writing skills. A simple language teaching method, again, would keep the learner fully at the centre and all work would revolve around him. A method made complex for the sake of ordering teaching techniques in a way not feasible in a particular situation would be a failure because only a pupil-oriented teaching method can teach the pupil proper language. Simplicity of method, therefore consists in organizing classroom experiences in such a way as to achieve maximum benefits by means of minimum techniques.

As a result, any simple method will be functionally feasible in the hands of any average teacher. The ultimate aim of methodics is to lay down the most practical guide-lines for the teacher to follow in order to make language teaching most effective. This can be achieved only if the method recommended means anything to the teacher in terms of what he is able to do in the classroom. Bilingual method is potential enough to germinate only those techniques which will be the least difficult and most effective provided the method is strictly adhered to. The fundamental simplicity of the method is made possible by the judicious use of the L_1. Owing to the strictly controlled use of the L_1 so much time is saved and effort is lessened that these precious resources can be channeled to the working of the four skills. The greatest simplicity of the method lies in the presentation of a structure or a set of vocabulary items where instead of the most complex demonstration and illustrative techniques, merely the equivalent of the mother-tongue is flashed across with a simple resulting on the faces of the pupils which makes sure that the meaning has gone home much faster than even the teacher's expectations through a word which is already a part of the pupils' *language experience*.

In the Indian context and against the background of the Indian languages, bilingual method is gaining greater acceptability and relevance. The argument is that a strict adherence to English language alone in the classroom is no longer possible in the present-day Indian context where the ideal English teacher is far from reality. Whether the bilingual method is the answer to the problem of English teaching in India is highly controversial. The principal reason for this being the average teacher's high-rate tendency to full back fully and unscrupulously on to the mother-tongue as is the case today. Perhaps, bilingual method in such circumstances would only be a licence for the full-fledged used of the L_1 and subsequently falling back again on to the grammar-translation way of teaching English. If kept within the recommended guide-lines, bilingual method will certainly prove effective provided the English atmosphere required so much in the classroom is fully maintained.

8
Communicative Language Teaching

1. Communicative Approach to Language Teaching

All classroom practices are controlled remotely by a variety of Approaches, determined by a specific procedural (methodological) framework that the teacher chooses and are realised finally by a set of techniques employed by him within that particular procedural framework. The syllabus which is essentially the guideline or the content framework for the teacher's work in the classroom is structural on the basis of the approaches that constitute the theoretical background. *A grammatical syllabus* in its strictest sense aims at the teaching of the formal grammar of English and helps the learner have the knowledge of the formal grammar of English. The learner will know what the meaning of simple present tense is even if the will not be in a position to construct sentences in the tense. The teaching material will be organised around formal aspects of grammar. *A structural syllabus aims* on the other hand at the teaching of functional grammar *i.e.,* the structures of English and helps the learner develop proficiency in the four skills of the language: listening, speaking, reading and writing. The learner will know how exactly to produce grammatical sentences and use them contextually even if he may not be in a position to offer grammatical explanations to the sentences he makes. The teaching material will thus be organised around the grammatical structure of English.

A situational syllabus aims at creating in the classroom situations in which the native speakers employ English as a language of communication. The learner will obtain proficiency over the skills of English by using the language as organised around a situation as the focal point of work in the classroom. The focus is thus not a grammatical or vocabulary item but a life-situation in which the language is employed. *A notional-functional syllabus as envisaged* by Dell Hymes (1971) aims at organising all teaching of English around the notional vs functional categories of the language. The syllabus will not be centered on structures and vocabulary, but structures and vocabulary will be generated by notional categories such as 'Time, Relation, Movement, Direction and Obligation,' and by functional categories such as 'making requests, expressing, regrets, asking pardon, and making promises'. The learner procures mastery over the language skills with the language work centered on these notional-functional categories.

A communicative syllabus as contrasted to all the approaches above combine a number of aspects mentioned above and aims at organising all teaching of English around what has come to be called *communicative tasks*. This is an *approach* because it is axiomatic and functions as the springboard for methodology which in turn defines a set of classroom techniques. A communicative syllabus for teaching English does not consist of a list of structures, or notional or functional categories as the above syllabuses are, but the whole thing becomes a *task-oriented teaching*. Communicative tasks assume a special meaning in communicating language teaching. The learner is provided simulated learning situations in the classroom or outside of it. This incorporates situational language teaching and employs situations as the spring-board for concrete language components for communicative purposes. Techniques that are part of other approaches are reorganised to enable learners effectively coordinate a communicative situation.

It is envisaged that the situations and tasks for which the native speaker employs English can function as the focal point around which learning can take place. This is looked upon as the most natural classroom practice that learners are capable of. They find themselves face-to-face with a set of tasks in the form of any activity for which they have to coordinate English. By undertaking the specific set of tasks which the teacher initiates in the classroom and by establishing a link between the task as a feature of experience on the one hand and the form, meaning and use of the corresponding language on the other. Communicative language teaching stands out from the rest of language teaching approaches in its emphasis on the *communicative role* of language for which English is primarily meant.

Another significant aspect of communicative language teaching is that is places high premium on the *communicative nature* of language. What language is to teach? The question for the classroom can be answered in a variety of ways: standard English vs diatectical English, formal English vs informal English, general English vs professional English or English for specific purposes, formal English vs Colloquialism and the list of language varieties can go on. The communicative classroom teaching is called on to choose that form of language which suits the learner most to carry out his day-to-day functions of communication. These functions are simulated in the classroom through tasks and role-playing. The language of the textbook is given an added dimension of informalism and colloquialism so that the language will function as a vehicle of communication for which it is meant. The language thus learned in the classroom comes handy to the learner out in the community for whatever communicative purposes he is called on to use it.

2. Emphasis on Communicative Categories

D.A. Wilkins envisages three different levels of meaning which constitute what we know as the semantic component of language: 1. Grammatical meaning. 2. Modal meaning and 3. Contextual meaning. The grammatical meaning of language is what we know as the 'propositional meaning' *i.e.*, the exact semantic dimension of a given sentence in which the logical truth of the sentence lies. This constitutes the *first level meaning* which is not drawn from the contextual setting of the sentence but is available to the listener/reader even if the sentence is given in isolation.

1. Oh ! afterall, John knows everything.

2. We shall pay up the whole amount today itself.

Sentences 1 and 2 at once reveal to any listener/reader the grammatical/propositional meaning without reference to any contextual setting. These sentences are first of all understood by the listener with reference to these meanings which is decoded from the sentences on the basis of the direct semantic contents of the lexical items. Hence this level of meaning is called grammatical or propositional meaning. This level of meaning is thus not derived from any aspects other than what sentences as such objectively stand for.

The second level of meaning is called *modal meaning*. This includes all aspects and dimensions of meaning that are added to an utterance from *the attitudes* of the speaker. The basic grammatical meaning can be completely altered by any attitude that the speaker may assume from time to time. The sentences given above 1 and 2 can mean exactly the opposite of their grammatical meanings when spoken in an attitude scorn or sarcasm.

1. Oh! afterall, John knows everything!

2. We shall pay up the whole amount today itself !

In an attitude of sarcasm sentence 1 would mean 'John known nothing' and 2. would mean 'we shall never pay up the whole amount.' Our attitudes from time to time can colour our language in such a way that not only do the utterances assume new dimensions but also totally change the meanings.

The third level of meaning is the *contextual meaning*. The distinction between the second and third levels are made only for the sake of theoretical clarity. Otherwise the two are closely linked. Contextual meanings are semantic dimensions that sentences assume in contexts other than the ordinary. This is central to ordinary speech as well as poetry. *Poetic deviations* are highly contextualised. The grammatical norms of the prose language become the background against which the poet applies grammatical and lexical deviations. The semantic context alone can justify the occurrence of such highly poetic usages. Contextual meanings are thus dimensions of meanings which a specific socio-cultural, poetic, or communicative context adds to a sentence.

These are primarily *communicative contexts*. Each communication is an event, a *communicative event* from a socio-linguistic viewpoint. The meanings that our sentences assume are determined by the communicative context in which the sentences are given shape to. In written language this context constitutes *the discourse* in which the sentence is used. In spoken and conversational language this context can be some form of non-verbal behaviour or, again, the oral discourse itself which the speaker himself or the speakers are developing.

1. Please do it the way I have already shown you.

2. The shape of the box is non of my concern.

These two sentences are grammatically correct and unambiguous but what is meant can only be known from a much larger discourse context.

3. The Role of Communicative Competence

Dell Hymes (1971) proposes in equal terms a level of linguistic competence which he calls communicative competence. Wilkins's communicative categories include all that the speaker does with language, as against what we report through language. In traditional teaching we made grammatical categories the very centre of all classroom practices. But today we proposes to have the classroom teaching of English to be centered on communicative categories such as those mentioned in Section 1. Dell Hymes outlines a theory of communicative competence which is complementary to Chomsky's theory of grammatical competence (1965). While grammatical competence covers the internalised knowledge only of the grammar of the language for the production of correct sentences, communicative competence includes a much wider perspective including all aspects of speech that render communication what it is.

Communicative language teaching relates language to the actual world of the speaker-listener. Language teaching becomes a thoroughly functional affair with not only formal linguistic, but also para-linguistic, extra-linguistic and pragmatic considerations brought upon the teaching of English. The functions of naming, wishing, promising, asking excuses, admonishing and directing assume a new dimension in the classroom and become the central aspects of English teaching. Children are taught to think through the language rather than translate things to the second language. All situational language teaching takes on a new communicative dimensions.

4. Communicative Event and Rules of Use

Communicative language teaching is essentially creative, purposeful and task-oriented. The grammatical rules of English language are determined by the nature of the language itself but the *rules of use* and the *appropriateness* of the use are determined by the speech community. Communicative language teaching puts a high premium on the deepest human significance of language learning, that language is a means to social interaction, that language is a vehicle to interpersonal communion by the members of society. It suggests the transition from an automatic, mechanical and formalistic perspectives to a more creative, purposeful, learner-centered and communication-oriented teaching of English as a second language. What is important is whether an expression in English is formally possible or correct within the strict framework of a rigid grammar but whether the expression is *actually used* by the speech community. If so that expression should find a place in the classroom. The very goal of a communicative language teaching based on 'communicative competence' is to show the learner of English ways in which the grammatically possible, acceptable and appropriate are linked to interpret actually occurring socio-cultural and contextual behaviour within the framework of communication as an event. It means the learner in the classroom should be in a position to identify that language which actually occur in the midst of the speech community from the mass of language material that the teacher or the instructional material offer him from time to time. If this can be done then second language learning can never become an airy-fairy thing.

Communicative language teaching is conceived of in the present context as an approach to the teaching of English as a

Second Language. This would mean that this approach should generate a set of classroom procedures linked to every skill and component of language as well as a set of *classroom techniques* that will implement that basic principles of communicative approach. What should be done is to integrate into the various methods of teaching English classroom techniques based on communicative language teaching. As we have seen techniques constitute well-defined and systematic activities by the teacher to help the pupil understand and use English language within the framework of a particular method. The following could be the *organisation* of techniques according to the aspects and skills of English language.

5. Classroom Techniques for Communicative Teaching

Communicative Approach to classroom teaching equips the teacher of English with a set of classroom techniques to implement its principles. We may call these *communicative techniques* for classroom teaching. Within the methodological framework of communicative language teaching the teacher in the classroom decides to organise a set of techniques for the learner ' to do things in English', and to learn communicative functions in the using of English. Communicative teaching proposes the following classroom techniques just as structural teaching of English makes use of a set of techniques to teach the Structures of English Language.

1. *Group Work* has been thought of as one of the best methods for initiating communicative activities. There is no end to the variety of techniques that can form part of groupwork. The objective is to help the learners use the new language function in a small group, talk to one another, ask questions, find patterns that will constitute the correct answers, reorganise the answers for the use of different patterns and practice and use of *communicative expressions* that are essentially part of conversational English. Expressions and polite forms. Such as the following should form part of the learner's language through group activities: God morning, Sir; What can I do for you?; How can I be of help to you?; Could you tell me what the matter is?; I wonder what I can do for you; Just a minute, Sir; Excuse me, but......; Certainly, Sir; Just a minute, Sir; Could you pass that book to me?; Would you want me to come with you to the shop?; Is there

anything that I can do for you?; May I have your pen for a while?; Well, I don't think I should tell you this; I don't know if I should tell you this; You're most welcome to join us; Can I take leave of you; please?; I think I must join you later; Excuse me for the awful delay; I certainly didn't mean it, that way; Oh! Your help is most welcome; You don't know how thankful I am; I'm sorry for making this remark...... The list of such expressions is certainly endless. Communicative language teaching expects to take care of such fine shades of what we have called the communicative event.

2. *Pair-Work* is another very effective device for initiating communicative activities. Here the class will be divided into groups of two as they are reacted in the class. No re-arrangement is necessary. Inter-questioning as a technique is the best for pair work. One will ask the question based on the materials given and the second will provide the answer. Then they swap roles and do the same. The greatest advantage of pair-work is that it is a very simple-method that the whole class is kept active and every individual gets the necessary involvement.

3. *Role Play* is another very dynamic technique that lies at the core of communicative language teaching. The individual in society is essentially a role-player. Language is employed as a vehicle to give expression to these roles in a variety of ways. In communicative language teaching these natural roles in society are simulated in the classroom and the learner uses language to give expression to the same features of experience. In otherwords role-play enables the learner to simulate in the classroom situations and activities for which the native speaker uses English in their real life situations.

4. *Dramatization* includes a variety of activities right from simple enactment of piece of conversation upto same form of a skit in which whole short theme can be handled. This is highly activity-oriented. The language function that has newly been introduced can be enlarged and worked out into some form of dramatisation. While role-play is simple dramatisation can be complex. In either case the important aspect is the communicative function that is practiced.

5. *Miming* : While miming and role-play have things in common miming can generate greater fun if worked out well. It miming as classroom technique one or more students engage in a process of imitating some character, say, a barber, a smith, a doctor, a typist etc.... The teacher guides the imitation by the student or does the imitation himself while at the same time a student is asked to interpret and say what is being done. Here is non-verbal behaviour sequence to translation into English language. Miming can easily be carried out in the classroom context.

6. *Reporting Observation*: There are many ways of carrying out communicative activities by reporting observations of several kinds. This is a highly practical activity. The learners can be asked to (a) measure the size of things and rooms and report the measurement in English, (b) Calculate or solve problems and report the findings in English, (c) observe games and report to the class how the games went on, (d) observe nature and report to the group what they see in a field, river side, at a picnic sport etc., (e) observe the traffic and report what is happening in a street, and (f) observe an experiment in the laboratory and report in English the details of the experiment.

7. *Inter-questioning* : Questioning is a classroom techniques that the teacher makes use of, while inter-questioning is the same activity done by the pupils with a different purpose. A groupwork or a pair work can integrate this technique. The difference lies in the fact that both groupwork and pair-work do not enable the whole class to listen to what is happening as the work is done only within the group. On the otherhand inter-questioning as thought of here is carried out before the whole class. The questions can be written on a piece of paper and the pupils can look at those and ask the questions. Everytime the question is asked and answer provided we are creating the language atmosphere that our classrooms are very badly in need of.

8. *Work on Pictures* : Pictures, sketches, and charts can be employed for very creative use in communicative language teaching. At this stage these are not used for the technique of pictorial illustration but as a teaching aid and constitute the material on which language can be generated. A group or a pair can be asked to produce communicative sentences and expressions from the

picture. The picture of a fair here substitutes for a real fair. While to talk on a real fair the pupils have gone to, their imagination needs to be exerted. The picture brings home a reality which cannot otherwise be brought home in all its details. Each group can work on different pictures, and attempt some kind of a description which should involve questions and answers related to the matter on the picture.

8. *Work on Models*: Models of any kind can help generate communicative language material. The three dimensional presentation of any model becomes more realistic and the work becomes more down-to-earth. Models can be brought to classrooms or pupils can be taken to places where such models are available. The model of a building, something that can easily available can generate excellent language. Such a model brings before the eyes of the pupils a whole three dimensional experience whose features cannot otherwise be brought together for purposes of observation and analysis.

9. *Making a Guess* : It is possible to do creative and imaginative language work through activities such as passing a packet and making a guess. Each pupil has to make a guess and say what the packet contains and give a description of the nature of the thing through short sentences. It could also be any form of making a guess, provided language is produced. This could either be done before the whole class or in group work.

10. *Talking about John* : This involves a pupil attempting to construct sentences with the teachers help about a friend he chooses. In such cases the friend should be known to him so that a few details of 'what he is' could be worked out. Again the purpose here is to enable the pupils to talk about their friends which constitutes fine material for communicative language practice.

11. *Reporting T.V./Video Scenes* : At a time when television has become part and parcel of modern life this technological device becomes one of the best tools for communicative language practice. If T.V. is available to the pupils at the school or in the classroom, the *silent visual stream* can become excellent material for communicative language activity. Slow motion, still frames

or even normal visual stream on the monitor can form the background for the pupils to report to the whole class or for the whole class to undertake writing on what is going on. T.V. scenes can become the feeding ground for miming, role play as well as dramatisation.

12. *Listen and Say* : The Tape recorder can be brought to the aid of communicative language teaching, either as part of the regular language laboratory or in the regular classroom: (a) recorded dialogues can be taken up for further classroom practice; (b) one character in a conversation can be played to the pupil and he can function on his own as the second character; (c) listen to the first part of a conversation and the pupils can dramatise the latter part in an imaginative manner; (d) play to the class a passage (preferably a story) and the pupils can produce orally or in writing the full story or part of it in their own simple sentences; and (e) a biographical sketch can be given in third person on the tape and the pupils convert the same into a biographical sketch in the first person. In the same manner we can introduce a communicative manner structural changes of tenses, voices, reported speech, interrogative patterns and so on.

13. *Overhead Projector* : Communicative language teaching can be made all the more effective if the teacher has the facility to make use of an overhead projector. The facility of an overhead projector to provide amplified visual presentation of diagrams, sketches and all forms of transparencies the teacher of English can employ several techniques for effective classroom teaching using such a projector. The major advantage is that actual *language material* can be projected for the whole class: dialogues in part or full, frames for composition, outlines of stories, cues for a variety of classroom tasks, pictures on which sentences can be developed, and a variety of *roles* with which the pupils will identify themselves and undertake role-play or dramatisation.

6. Materials for Communicative Language Teaching

The major objective of communication language teaching as we have seen is to help the learner *make concrete use* of the language and do things through the language rather than learning about the structures of the language. The learner should be able to carryout a variety of *communicative tasks* in which English is made use of. The task before the teacher therefore is to prepare such materials as to attain this objective. Whatever teaching materials that he prepares whether (a) instructional material or (b) test material, should reflect this fundamental quality. Instructional materials prepared within the framework of structural approach are centered on the structures of English and aim at delineating those structures either for the skill of speech or writing. Materials for communicative language teaching centres on the other hand on what the learner can do through the language.

The following *categories of communication* can go into the making of both a *communicative syllabus* and *communicative instructional material* :

Asking the Way : Could you tell me the way to......
Excuse me but, is this the way to.....
How can I reach the bus station....

Apologising : I am sorry for stepping on your toes......
I am awfully sorry for...
Oh, I am really sorry for.. .

Acceptance : I am grateful you have.....
I feel obliged to.....
Thank you very much for. ...

Agreement : I agree to abide by your instructions
We agree that we meet on...
We agree to pay him....

Accusation : I am sure he did it
I feel sure that he is the one.....
We are sure that John....

Acknowledgment: We acknowledge that you are.....
We acknowledge that you have...
We recognise how accomplished...

Admonition : We warn you never again to...
They exhorted him to....
We advise you to take case of ....

Affirmation :	I declare that John has been....... You have asserted that John has..... They have maintained that.........
Consequence :	As a result of his intervention....... Consequently, he left the place. As a consequence, they have decided......
Contrast :	As against this I would like to..... In contrast to they insisted on...... If this is too simple then.......
Certainty :	I am indeed certain that...... He is sure to go there on Monday...... Make sure that he does it........ As compared to your statement........ This boy is indeed taller........ Why don't you try harder ?
Expressing : emotions	How said I feel you do not know ! I am overwhelmed at your concern.... Oh! How hard It tried, yet.....
Explanation :	To put more clearly.... As far as the details are concerned.... We demand an explanation from you.....
Emphasising :	This is indeed the truth... You cannot do it in any way other than..... I am convinced that you will...
Frequency :	He does it ~~of~~ten. Never have I seen him doing it. They have always been going then.
Insistence :	I want you to complete.... You must make sure that.... They should at all cost go there.....
Invitation :	I have been invited to... You are most cordially invited to..... John is most welcome to....

Promises :	I promise to give the money back. We shall pay you the money back. John promised to visit him...
Permission :	You may leave the place.... May I obtain some money..... Can I sit here and do the work?
Questioning :	Have you broken these glasses? Tell me, if you wrote this letter. How much time would you take to...
Restriction :	You are not allowed to... Let him work only upto Monday. Do not cross this line.
Regrets :	I regret my absence at.... I am sorry I cannot..... We regret our inability to....

The list above constitutes only a few of the communicative functions that go into the making of a communicative syllabus as well as materials for communicative teaching of English. What we aim at in the preparation of such materials is to organise the structures and vocabulary of English around the communicative functions which the language projects. These functions are embedded in and represented by lexical items such as promises, permission, an restriction. Under these labels we attempts to bring together all the sentences patterns and grammatical items that go into the making of English language. Materials preparation for communicative language teaching is very specialised task and should project and fundamental aim that we have on hand. It loses all its purpose if such syllabus and materials cannot be properly distinguished from structural syllabuses and materials. The teacher of English should be convinced of this aim and these characteristics of communicative teaching so that teaching English can be made all the more effective.

7. Communicative Teaching as Task Centered

It has already been mentioned that the central component of communicative language teaching is *the task*, a notion that makes this approach a remarkable one. The atmosphere of the traditional classroom is exclusively of the regional language with English hardly figuring in any where except in reading and writing. The structural approach wedded to the direct method attempts to avoid the use of the regional language and develop speech habits without resorting to the regional language. The revised structural approach on the other hand is cut off from direct method and focuses on the teaching of functional grammar by helping the learner use the grammatical structures both in speech and in writing. The aim is no longer in the exclusive development of the listening speaking skill but in the overall development of all the skills.

The principal contribution of communicative approach then is its stress on task-oriented teaching of English. An attempt is made to divert attention from the structural aspects of English and concentrate on what English can do in functional situations. Not that the functional aspects of English is in any way a new thing. Its role has long since been recognised in the teaching of English. But never in the history of English language teaching has the communicative functions been so much brought to fucus as with communicative language teaching.

The teacher in the communicative classroom uses the communicative functions of language as the springboard for language practice. He devices a variety of tasks that the pupils are asked to do in the class or in the school premises. The pupils are asked to 1. measure objects, 2. make models, 3. prepare projects, 4. make enquiries, 5. report things, 6. analyse problems, 7. make designs and plans, 8. make calculations, 9. describe objects, make proposals and 10. organise activities. English as a language of communication is employed for all these. The task need not therefore by anything material and physical, it should ' make the pupils do' things in the language including the functions that are of merely verbal nature. Communicative language teaching keeps also role-play at the very centre an thus helps the learner do things rather than merely learn verbal language from the pages of the textbook. Language teaching becomes a highly contextualised affair; the teacher can no longer hide behind the pages of the textbook and leave the learner to his usual fate. The communicative classroom calls for teachers of highly dynamic character or else we lapse back into the same morose texting that is the usual fate of our classrooms.

9
Language Content and Kinds of Lessons

1. The Structure of English and Kinds of Lessons

It is not required that every English teacher should be a linguist or a psychologist. All the same, more is expected of the teacher than of any other professional as his is a characteristic vocation. Mostly the English teacher undertakes to teach a lesson without fully knowing the implications the lesson has on the learner's language acquisition as well as without knowing what specific aspects of the *language content* he wants the pupils to acquire. Every lesson in English has specific relations to some aspect of the content of the language, or rather as we shall be examining in detail, every aspect of English as a language is capable of yielding a specific kind of lesson within the overall framework of language learning.

In present-day circumstances with all the emphasis put on the written form of language, we no longer need to consider language as exclusively speech. An analysis of the structure of language would yield a variety of elements which usually form part of a course in linguistics. Before anything else is undertaken, it is worthwhile to keep in mind that it is *a language* as such that the teacher helps the learners acquire, not any of its sub-systems in particular. At the same time, the teaching of the language in a classroom would mean a diversification of its subsystems for purposes of functional convenience and more effective teaching. English language, consequently is a system which consists of the following sub-components :

(1) Language is *competence and performance.* Competence is the 'built-in ability' of the native speaker which forms the 'theoretical base' of the functional-shoots : listening, speaking, reading and writing, all of which involve the actual exercise of the linguistic competence. The actual exercise of the language by means of the four skills, we call, performance. In other words we may identify the performance of English with the exercise of the four language skills.

(2) The knowledge of English language would mean two things : (i) *theoretical knowledge*, and (ii) *possession of the skills.* Theoretical knowledge of a language could be by means of another language or it may be by means of the ability only to read and write. This will include all formal studies on the language such as grammar, its history, linguistics, and literature. The language skills consist in the actual possession of the language by means of (i) competence, and (ii) performance. The possession of the skills would mean, thus, the knowledge and exercise of the same.

(3) Linguistic performance would mean, again, two things: *Speech* and *writing*, which in terms of language content yield *spoken language* and *written language*. Spoken language, in turn, apparently consists of *sounds* and *meanings*, while written language consists of *graphemes* and *meanings*.

(4) Language in its spoken as well as written forms is structured of two sets of elements : (i) structures and (ii) lexis. Structures in turn consists of (i) *structural items* and (ii) *sentence patterns*. Structural items (known as function words or grammar words) go into the ordering of the lexical items (also known as vocabulary items) in a sentence of the language. While structural words and sentence patterns are the concern of the grammarian, the lexis which from the bulk of a dic-

tionary are the concern of the lexicographer who is specialized in the making of a dictionary. While articles, prepositions, conjunctions, auxiliaries, pronouns etc. fall in the category of structural words, nouns, verbs, adjectives and adverbs which possess a *definable conceptual content* are grouped under lexical items (known also collectively as the *lexicon* of the language). Tenses, voices, reported speech, clauses, interrogative forms, forms of sentences etc. go under sentence patterns.

(5) Spoken and Written language consist of several subcomponents : (i) sounds (letters), (ii) morphemes, (iii) words, (iv) phrases, (v) clauses, (vi) sentences and (vii) discourses larger than the sentence. All these except sounds and letters possess the property of *meanings* which further consist of sub-elements called, *conceptual units.*

(6) Thus, language would, again be thought of as consisting of two major facets : (i) *expression*, and (ii) *content*. By expression we mean the extrinsic layer of language which consists of all forms from sounds to discourses as mentioned in (5); while the content of the language is the intrinsic layer known by the term 'meanings' studied under that area of linguistics known as *semantics*.

(7) Just as language is expression and content, it is also *comprehension* and *content*. While it is expression and content for the speaker, language is comprehension and content for the listener. These have significant teaching implications as will be discussed later.

(8) Language as expression consists of *oral expression* and *written expression*. These are also know as *oral communication* and *written communication*. Language as comprehension, by contrast, consists of *listening comprehension* and *reading comprehension*.

The structure of English language, as we have examined, is complex enough for an investigator to spend a life-time on it. The

English teacher in the classroom, faced with the task of teaching English on the basis of a '*teaching unit*' as the centre around which to move, will need to see language from several of the view-points examined above. English language as a set of sounds, and their combination in set patterns, the teacher is required to teach *Pronunciation*; the spoken form of English language with all its phatic expression, patterns of stress and intonation, as well as forms of oral expression call for the teaching of *Spoken English*. The English teacher has the major task of teaching the structures of English through *Structure (Grammar) Lessons*. This will form the major bulk of teaching English at any level, especially in the case of L_2 learners of English in L_1 schools. Again, lexis consists of the major bulk of language both in speech and in writing. The lexical items occurring in a lesson in the textbook will be treated in *Vocabulary lessons*. Reading and writing are considered the third and fourth skills of language. But reading can be for various purposes. *Intensive Reading* lessons aim at helping the learners read some written material analytically and in detail taking into consideration all aspects of the language. *Extensive Reading* lessons aim at the development of the fast reading skill and comprehension of the material in general. Again, there are compositions of various kinds aiming at helping the learner compose and give shape to discourses of various kinds. *Oral composition* lessons help the learner build discourses orally without any visual aid of a picture. In *Picture* composition lessons the pupils develop an oral discourse on the basis of picture which provides all the material in visual modality. The climax consists in *written composition* where on the basis of what has been discussed, the pupils write a discourse in the form of one or more paragraphs, a dialogue etc. Lastly, there is that aesthetic aspect of language, poetry, which the teacher of English at any level cannot forget. *Appreciation lessons*, thus, are meant to enable the pupils to get into the mood of looking at language as art and a mosaic of sound patterns.

Apart from the fact that every lesson has a core in terms of the language content as we have seen, every lesson consists of a predominant skill as the fundamental aim of these lessons in English is the development of language skills. Every lesson is aimed at the development of one skill or other along with the pupils' acquaintence with the content matter of the lesson. Again it must be emphasized that the teaching of separate kinds of lessons arising from a unit as well as the teaching of the skills are all ultimately aimed at the development and mastery of one and the same thing : English language, both in its written and spoken forms. It will be, therefore, the concern of the sections to place every lesson in English in relation to its language content on the one hand, and the skills on the other so that all this could be conceived as a *unified experience* amidst the great diversity of linguistic units.

2. Speech-Forms and Spoken English Lessons

Language is speech, and the teaching of English language would mean the teaching of the spoken English. It does not mean that English as a set of spoken forms exist separately from English as a set of written forms. The two sets of forms intercept in such a way that there are more elements common to both than there are differences because it is one and the same English language which is realized in speech and in writing. All the same, one may not deny that spoken English has a uniqueness which is characterized by several features of the language. For this matter, it is not possible to identify spoken English with written English apart from the fact that the two form separate skills of English language. Teaching spoken English, therefore, requires separate treatment in the teaching of English as L_2.

By a Spoken English lesson we do not mean any listening-speaking lesson where the skills of listening and speaking will be predominant. By this we mean the teaching of elements which are peculiar to spoken English only and do not form part of written English. There are several features characteristic to spoken English that form the content of a Spoken English lesson. The teaching of *pronunciation* forms the major bulk of spoken English lessons. Aspects of pronunciation, especially in English by contrast to the orthography of English, are so important that the learning of spoken English primarily means the learning of the pronunciation of English words, phrases, and sentences. For this reason, pronunciation lessons could be conceived as a unit separate from other aspects of spoken English. A pronunciation lesson would consist of a body of teaching techniques (Ch. 7, Sec. 6 of

'Teaching English in India') which are exclusively mean to help the learners acquire the correct pronunciation of the consonants, vowels, diphthongs, triphthongs, sound sequences (clusters) and words of English language. These are classes exclusively used for purposes of teaching a particular set of items of pronunciation.

A Spoken English lesson would consist of a body of teaching techniques to enable the learners of a particular level to acquire mastery over the use of items of spoken English such as the following : (1) patterns of intonation in English, (2) stress of English words which occur in day-to-day use as well as those that the learners are expected to pick up, (3) the proper use of weak forms in English, (4) forms of questioning, (5) the phatic expressions, such as the use of *please*, which occur in every day use, (6) ways of *greeting* people of various walks of life etc. A lesson in spoken English is structured so as to take care of any one of these or other aspects of spoken English. Even though there are times when the teacher can take care of some of these during his regular teaching, such Spoken English lessons will be of great value in countries like India where spoken English is the most difficult area of students to master.

3. Structures and Grammar Lessons

The structuralists were right when it was emphasized that language consists fundamentally of structures and that the teaching of a foreign language should consist of teaching the structures of the language *i.e.* in helping the learners actively use the structural elements of the foreign language. Teaching grammar which was confined to a few isolated classes in the grammar-translation method has now become the centre of teaching English in schools. Structural items and sentence patterns are so fundamental that every English lesson is built around a particular item. A lesson in the text-book at the learner's disposal is a highly potential *Unit* for the learning of the language. All things could begin from this Unit, as aspects of language learning evolving out of it. The lesson as a language teaching Unit is representative or the embodiment of some structure.

Consequently, the structure embedded in a lesson is the very starting point of a series of highly interrelated lessons, as we are examining it throughout the present chapter. L_2 learning is considered chiefly the learning of the structures of the language, but under the present setup, and unlike in grammar-translation system, the structures of English are not committed to memory in terms of the rules of grammar, but the pupils are expected to *internalize* the structures by means of practice and constant acquaintances with the meaning and actual use of the structures of English. Therefore, instead of teaching 'grammar' as isolated lessons without any logical relation to the textbook, the teacher of English is expected to begin all the teaching of a Unit from the teaching of the structure concerned, carry on the revision of the structures in the lessons which follow, and enable the learners ultimately to employ the structures in the construction of discourses which in turn will be useful for purposes of communication.

The structure lesson which will be the first lesson to follow from a teaching Unit is, thus to be very well distinguished from the traditional 'grammar teaching'. As one can find the entire scope and framework of a structure lesson in detail in 'Teaching English in India', it suffices here to say that the major part of teaching English as a second language consists of teaching the Structures of English. The structures of English would include, as we have seen, (i) *the structural items* such as articles, prepositions, conjunctions, auxiliaries, comparatives, superlatives, question-tags etc.; and (ii) *sentence patterns* such as the tenses, passive voice, question forms, adverbs clauses, adjective clauses, reported speech etc. Teaching all other lessons including reading and writing is based on the work done of particular structures in class. The structure is therefore the central aspect of a teaching Unit.

4. Lexis and Vocabulary Lessons

If a Spoken English lesson takes care of the specific features of spoken English, and a Structure lesson teaches the structure used in the teaching unit, then a *Vocabulary* lesson teaches the lexical items newly used in the unit. The textbook is constructed in a characteristic manner. Just as every lesson presents a new structure and revises one ore more structures taught right before, every lesson as a teaching unit is constructed by means of some particulars register of the language. A register consists of lexical items intimately related to one another, centered on and generating from a particular life situation such as a profession, an occupation, a place, or an action of some significance in a community. A *hospital* would generate words such as doctor, nurse, medicine, patient, operation, injection etc. which are characteristically related to the life situation. The same would be true of professions such as those of a lawyer, a teacher, or an engineer, or occupations such as those of a farmer, a carpenter, a goldsmith or a businessman. Every such life situation would yield a closely linked *set of lexical items* which can be worked out together into a discourse in the form of a descriptive paragraph, a story or a piece of conversation. What is significant here is that the teaching unit presented in the text book for work in the classroom consists of such a register worked out into a set of descriptive paragraphs, a story or a piece of conversation.

At the same time, such a lesson in the textbook consists of lexical items which have already been introduced in preceding lessons, as well as there are quite a specified number of lexical items which are newly introduced. In doing so the textbook writer intends, on the one hand to acquaint the pupils with a set of new vocabulary items and on the other, help them revise the vocabulary items repeated in the lesson. The lesson is supposed to contain both active vocabulary for expression, and recognition vocabulary meant only for comprehension purposes. The *expression vocabulary* should be so mastered as to be at the disposal of the child for active use in speech and writing; but the *recognition vocabulary* would be of help in listening and reading which involve an approximation of what the agent possesses with what is spoken or written. Just as the structures of English require separate treatment, by means of a specific lesson the learners can be helped to work on the lexical items sufficiently enough to make it an active part of their language store.

5. Reading Material and Reading Lessons

Structures and vocabulary are the raw-material which go into the making of a teaching-unit that we call a lesson in the textbook. The teacher after having completed work with the structures embedded in the unit and the vocabulary by means of which the unit is built up, has the next task to use the unit as *reading lesson*. A teaching unit prepared within the guidelines of the structural approach does not consist of an extract from any classical writing as the language, but the unit (lesson) is specially constructed around a situation employing the structures and vocabulary recommended for that unit. Attempts are made in such a unit to meet the following requirements : (1) a lesson is built up consisting of paragraphs or conversation so as to enable the pupils to use the same for purposes of comprehension; (2) the lesson is made suitable to the level for which it is used by using only the kind of language as well as content material which will be within the grasping power of the particular level; (3) it is seen that the number of new words used is specific and that the most recent set of words taught is revised more, and (4) the content of the lesson *i.e.* the ideas expressed are neither beyond the grasping power nor below the 'take-in' level of the pupils. Too familiar material presented in too simple a language would not be a challenging reading material for any level.

The unit is used as a reading lesson with a specific view to developing the skill of reading material in English. By reading we do not mean reading aloud, as will be understood in the chapter on Reading. By reading we mean silent reading only whatever be the proximate purpose of such silent reading. In the Reading lesson we aim at two things : *comprehension* and the *reading speed*. These two factors are borne in mind while building up the passage for reading. Since the passage is to be read within a limited period only, a too lengthy passage would not serve the purpose. Again, if it consists of expressions and patterns which the pupils have not studied, the passage would be considered the most inadequate because comprehension cannot be achieved of such a passage as well as every strange word or expression would be a hindrance for the pupils while reading. Just as *speaking* and *listening* consist of several sub-habits, *reading* silently requires the development of a number of mechanisms which we shall later be calling 'the mechanics of reading'. The lesson in the textbook furnishes the pupils with a systematically prepared material for purposes of developing the mechanics of reading with a view to achieving greater comprehension and faster reading in present-day circumstances when fast reading has become a great requirement.

6. Discourse-building and Composition Lessons

The L_2 learners of English master a structure of English in terms of its meanings and uses of a set of lexical items by means of which the structure can be effectively used in a particular situation, and reads a passage which is structured of the grammatical items and the vocabulary. But the *learning of English* through a *unit* does not stop there. The learner is further led to make use of his knowledge of the structure and the vocabulary for constructing language units bigger than a sentence which we call *discourses*. Ability in constructing isolated sentences using the structure and the vocabulary is not the ends of language learning. The language is full of representations of life situations; the pupils are required to express themselves within the framework of situation. For these reasons, composition is considered to be the climax of learning English : when the pupils will be able to *express themselves* in related sentences on a given situation.

As the way language is expressed could be in a descriptive or narrative paragraph, or a piece of conversation, it is found better to call the same a *discourse* rather than a paragraph. The student of English language can express himself in speech or in writing; in either the matter is composed in a specific manner. Consequently, we speak of *oral composition* and *written composition*. The aim is, again to develop the skills of oral and written expression. It is an attempt to get both the skills developed side-by-side so that the one will have greater bearing on the other.

In developing the skills of oral and written expression of a discourse, care is taken that both the discourses are thoroughly related. The aims are not to teach new aspects of language, but to help the learner organize what he has mastered upto a given time. For these reasons, it is recommended that the same discourse is used both for the *oral expression* and *written expression*. The pupils with the help of the teacher develops a discourse orally (Ch. 11 of 'Teaching English in India') and then later expresses the same material in writing. These features are discussed more in detail in the respective chapter on composition. But what is to be noted here is that oral expression and written expression are not isolated activities in a L_2 learning experience; they are so related to each other as well as to other language skill-based lessons that each is derived from a preceding lesson. If learning of spoken forms, and of a structure is the beginning, then composite oral and written expression will be the climax of learning experiences centered on a particular unit.

7. Poetry and Appreciation Lessons

Teaching English poetry in L_1 schools has been a very controvertial subject. The full implications of this problem are discussed in (Chapter 12, of 'Teaching English in India'). It has been traditionally held that the four basic skills of language are: listening, speaking, reading and writing. But this is only one view of language. Human language has dimensions greater than mere listening, speaking, reading and writing skills. The four skills have been defined as the functional off-shoots of linguistic competence. Human language has dimensions which cross the horizons of these functional off-shoots. Such dimensions of human language are its aesthetic, poetic, metaphysical and mystical applications. Eventhough these dimensions of language are rooted ultimately and concertedly in listening, speaking, reading and writing, language here crosses the horizons of its ordinary, communicational applications. Language is not an abstract system of symbols representing something with which it has no fundamental relationship, but human languages in trying to represent human experiences undergoes a process of unification with these experiences. For these reasons, language learning cannot be segregated from the linguistic dimensions such as poetry or literature.

All this would mean that there is an aspect very closely related to the four language skills, and this aspect is *appreciation*. Appreciation could be considered a language skill as authentic as the four basic skills, if we broaden the scope of the language skills. Appreciation can either be developed by means of listening to or reading the kind of language which is meant for the purpose. It is possible, therefore, to recite and appreciate, or read and appreciate poetry. Appreciation of poetry at higher levels of education such as the university could be called 'critical appreciation' when the individual person's critical judgement is called upon to enhance his sense of enjoyment. This is not the kind of appreciation that we wish our pupils to exercise. By means of various levels of poetry, beginning from mere *nursery rhymes* and going through full-fledged poetry, it is possible to develop in the learners of English a sense of appreciation for a language which is structured and organized for aesthetics effects. Teaching of poetry can be organized in such a way as to occur after the completion of one, two or three regular lessons in the textbook. If a particular textbook does not include poems of any kind, the teacher will have great pleasure in finding out and introducing good poems in the class, and thereby providing the pupils with chances for appreciating the way 'sound harmony' is exploited in English language through poetry. A full-fledged treatment of the aspects of teaching poetry is reserved for the chapter on the Teaching of Poetry. Teaching English as L_2 can be complete only by the teaching of poetry which initiates the learners to the aesthetic applications of English language.

10

Techniques of Teaching English

1. Techniques for Preliminary Work

A separate treatment of the teaching techniques for English is provided due to the fundamental role techniques play in the teaching of a language. It is not necessary for theoretical or practical purposes to broaden or narrow down the notion of techniques. In its broadest sense techniques consist of each and every activity a teacher undertakes soon after he enters the classroom until he leaves, to put across his teaching point. There cannot be a stage through out a class when the teacher does not do something to put across some language point, to teach or get some activity done in class. At the same time, in the narrow sense techniques consist of the *well-defined* and *select devices* the teacher voluntarily uses to provide the pupils necessary learning experiences. It is in this narrow sense that we have been using the term technique throughout the present work, and it is in the same sense that the term is used here. In this sense it is possible for us to distinguish the techniques the teacher uses at a particular teaching step. The following listing of *select techniques* is based on a grouping of (i) the various 'teaching Steps' on a criterion of (ii) the language skills. For instance Section 1. Techniques for Initial Work are sub-grouped under the teaching of structure, further sub-grouped under aspects such as (a) speech, (b) action, (c) pictures, (d) reading and (e) writing.

(A) Teaching of Spoken English

(a) Speech Techniques

There are several such techniques in which 'listening and speaking' are the main activities involved. These divisions are based on the characteristics of the technique that predominates, because all techniques are bound to involve some speech and action at some level.

1. *Questioning* : This is certainly the most resourceful technique at the teacher's disposal. Questioning is pure verbal behaviour, solely functioning on the realm of pure language, capable of evoking immediate verbal response from the pupils. Questioning maintains the abstract characteristic of language. Through out the present chapter the term 'questioning' refers only to the pure verbal behaviour of the teacher without any action or picture accompanying it unless such things are specified. The questions that the teacher asks may be of several major categories so far as the background is concerned depending on the manifold situations such as (i) pupil's outside experiences, (ii) classroom situations, and (iii) based on a picture. Questions from a linguistic view point are of two groups : (i) inverted or yes/no questions (*Is he going home* ?), and Wh questions (*where is he going* ?). The most significant thing to remember is the frame and the content of the question. The framing or the formation of a question in relation to the content is where the teacher often fails. Of course the frame and the content are not separable elements. The most proper question to be framed of a sentence as *Alex lives in the city of Bombay* is *Where does Alex live?* rather than *Who lives in Bombay ?* or any such question that does not make sense. The teacher while questioning should look for what is *new* in a sentence and what is somehow *given* previously or known to the pupils. *Alex* is the given (known) element and *Bombay* is supposed to be the new matter in relation to *Alex* in the given sentence.
2. *Look and Say* : As part of the revision work the teacher himself does or helps the pupils do certain activities. Other pupils watch the activities and frame sentences. This tech-

nique, as will be seen, is used for both revision and practice. The teacher asks *Simi* to show out her hands and seeing her empty hands *James* says: *She has no money in her hands.*

(b) Action techniques

1. *Do and say* : Here, the pupils are asked to perform certain activities and simultaneously frame sentences using the language item to be revised or practised. In fact 'dramatization' too involves the components of 'do and say' because in both the pupils are expected to perform certain actions and use the language in the given context. The major difference is that 'dramatization' involves a more organized and lengthy sequence of activity (*e.g.* conversation) then found in the teacher's 'demonstration', or the pupils' 'do and day', Sunil cleans the desk and says, *I am helping Liza clean her desk.*
2. *Dramatization*: Though dramatization is not recommended for revision work, it is possible to use the same if the teacher wishes so since revision to a great extent involves the use of the language in the same manner as practice does. There is great scope for the kind of freedom that the teacher may be allowed in this regard. Dramatization as a technique would mean any organized and sequential chain of activities such as a conversation using the structure or element of spoken English under consideration. Four pupils are asked to develop a conversation to use *Please, help do it* and *Thank you.* Dramatization is an excellent technique for revising or practising spoken English.
3. *Miming* : Miming as a technique involves imitation of some feature or situation such as the role of a barber in giving a hair-dress. Someone is asked to mimic the feature or situation and others verbalize the actions. Miming is an excellent device for any structure that has potency for on-the-spot description.

c) Picture techniques

1. *Look and say*: the pupils verbalize a situations given in a picture, and use the particular aspect of spoken English. During the revision teacher helps the pupils ask questions

of a one another (inter-questioning) in which the relevant aspect of spoken English is used.

Tom : Is Mr. Mohan walking across the road?

Lata: No, Mr. Mohan is standing on the road.

2. *Listen and Show* : The teacher verbalizes the situation given in a picture and asks the pupils to point it on the picture.

   Teacher: Miss White is wearing a black hat.

   Sunil : (shows Miss White on the picture).

(d) Reading techniques

1. *Read an say*: the pupils do certain exercises like 'sentence completion' presented on the chalk-board using the particular aspect of spoken English.

   a. Yes, I saw a bear——————————.
   b. Certainly, I cannot bear—————————.

2. *Reading aloud* : The teacher may occasionally make use of 'reading aloud' to provide practice in correct pronunciation of words, fluency of spoken English utterances and other aspects of spoken English.

B. Teaching Structure

(a) Speech techniques : 1. *Questioning* (as described in A. i), 2. Look and say (see A. ii). 3. Read and say (using the structure on the basis of a given written exercise, or using for instance, flash cards). 4. Inter-questioning which is initiated among the pupils, 5. Listen and say where the teacher uses exercise such as sentence completion for the pupils to revise the relevant structure

(b) Action techniques : 1. Demonstration (short actions, things, and gestures), 2. Do and say, 3. Miming, 4. Listen and show, 5. Listen and do, and 6. Dramatization.

(c) Picture techniques : 1. Look and say, 2. Listen and show, 3. Look and write (on the chalkboard), 4. Matching pictures with sentences and so on.

(d) Reading techniques : 1. Listen and read, 2. Read and do (by means of flash cards), 3. Read and say (using written exercises).

(e) Writing techniques : 1. Listen and write, 2. Look and write (using actions, 3. Read and writing.

C. Teaching Vocabulary

(a) Speech techniques : 1. Questioning 'to lead the pupils to the theme of the paragraph in which the new words are presented. 2. Inter-questioning (among the pupils) to help the pupils revise the structure of the unit. 3. Listen and say (the teacher speaks out a word and the pupils make sentences for revision purposes).

(b) Action techniques : 1. Do and say, used for revising the structure of the unit. 2. Look and say, used to obtain the verbal equivalents from the pupils. 3. Miming in which one imitates, and others verbalize the situation. 4. Listen and show, and 5. Listen and do where pupils perform actions as the teacher speaks.

(c) Picture techniques : 1. Look and say, 2. Listen and show, 3. Look and write, 4. Matching pictures with the verbal counterparts, 5. Pictures or sketch completion.

(d) Reading Techniques : 1. Read and say, 2. Listen and read, 3. Read and do (flash cards) etc.

(e) Writing Techniques : 1. Read and write, 2. Look and write, 3. Listen and write.

D. Teaching Reading

The Initial work of teaching reading may be done in three distinct ways : (i) *leading* to the theme of the lesson, (ii) *revision* of the structure in the unit, and (iii) *introducing* the new vocabulary, if a vocabulary lesson is not previously. It is left to the teacher to decide depending on the situation whether to takeup all the three in a sequence as part of the Initial Work or to take up only one or two of the three. But in the case of (i) and (ii) the techniques required are not different from what we have listed so far. In the case of (iii) reference should be made to the presentation part of the vocabulary lesson (2.C. of the present chapter).

E. Teaching Composition

LEARNING (RELATING) TECHNIQUES

(a) Speech techniques : 1. Questioning, 2. Inter-questioning,

3. Listen and say, 4. Narration.

(b) **Action techniques :** 1. Do and say, 2. Demonstration, 3. Dramatization.

(c) **Picture techniques :** 1. Look and say, 2. Listen and show, 3. Matching pictures with language items.

(d) **Reading techniques :** 1. Read and say, and 2. Tead and do (flash cards).

REVISION TECHNIQUES

(a) **Speech techniques :** 1. Questioning, 2. Look and say, 3. Listen and say, 4. Inter-questioning.

(b) **Action techniques :** 1. Do and say, 2. Listen and do.

(c) **Picture techniques :** 1. Look and say, 2. Listen and show, 3. Picture matching (see above).

(d) **Reading techniques :** 1. Read and say, 2. Read and do (flash cards).

NEW VOCABULARY

Please refer to the teaching techniques for introducing new vocabulary items (2.C. of present chapter).

F. Teaching Poetry

RELATING (LEADING) TECHNIQUES

(a) **Speech techniques :** 1. Questioning , 2. The use of the record-player for presenting a related and known poem, 3. Narration of a very short story, 4. Description of some familiar features.

(b) **Action techniques :** 1. Dramatization of some related event, 2. Do and say, 3. Miming to bring home some interesting and related theme or character.

(c) **Picture techniques :** 1. Dramatization against the background of a picture or sketches on the chalkboard, 2. Look and listen, 3. Questioning on the basis of a picture, 4. The use of match-stick drawings on the chalkboard to present a very short story as a thematic background to the poem, 5. Picture completion to build a short event or story to lead to the theme of the poem and relate them thematically.

(d) **Reading techniques** : 1. Presentation of a descriptive or narrative passage or dialogue on the chalkboard and questions of the same. The content of discourse is related to the content of the poem.

2. Techniques for Presentation

A. Teaching Spoken English

(a) **Speech Techniques** : 1. Verbal illustration *i.e.* the teacher presents the new material in verbal contexts only, 2. Listen and say, when the teacher requires the participation of the pupils for presenting certain structures, 3. Listen and do, when the teacher requires certain action by the pupils to put across the new structures. 4. Minimal pairs or pairs of words for presenting pronunciation.

(b) **Action techniques** : 1. Demonstration by means of objects and actions, 2. Miming is used where the new material requires imitative action, 3. Listen and do as part of presentation work, 4. Dramatization to teach aspects of conversation such as greeting formulas etc.

(c) **Picture techniques** : Listen and see, by means of pictures and sketches, 2. Association of action on pictures and then verbal counterparts, 3. Pictorial illustration of speech patterns.

(d) **Reading techniques** : Reading of specimen formulas, phrases and sentences from the chalkboard.

B. Teaching Structures

(a) **Action techniques** : 1. Demonstration by means of objects and actions ; 2. Miming is used when the new material requires sequential gesticulations to represent the significance; 3. Listen and do as part of the teacher's work where pupils are called for help; 4. Dramatization when the structure requires action-chains.

(b) **Speech techniques** : 1. Verbal illustration of the structure; the structure is presented through verbal contexts only; 2. Listen and say when the teacher requires the verbal participation of the pupils to present the new structure; 3. Listen and do, when the teacher needs certain actions on the part of the pupils to put across the new structural item.

(c) **Picture techniques :** 1. Pictorial illustration to bring home the meaning of some action or situation the picture represents; 2. Listen and see by means of pictures.

(d) **Reading techniques :** During presentation the pupils read and learn the visual presentation of the structures on the chalkboard.

C. Teaching Vocabulary

(a) **Speech techniques :** 1. Verbal illustration by means by sentences and situations, 2. Context cues when the meaning of a new word can be guessed from a verbal context; 3. Bilingual presentation in which the L_1 equivalent is presented; 4. Association of the new word with a sound counterpart; 5. Association of the new word with certain well know names of person, places or events.

(b) **Action techniques :** 1. Demonstration, 2. Look and listen when the teacher involves the pupils to do certain action in the class to teach some meaning; 3. Dramatization when the new word requires action-chains.

(c) **Pictures techniques :** 1. Pictorial illustration when the teacher drives home the meaning of a word by means of picture, sketch or a diagram; 2. Incomplete picture to help pupils make a guess and learn the meaning; 3. Mach-stick drawings to represent a situation on the chalkboard to teach some particular meaning.

(d) **Questioning** is used to help the pupils use the words in own sentences and at once consolidate the new learning that has taken place.

D. Teaching Reading

The Step 2 of a reading lesson (Intensive Reading) consists of the teacher's model reading. It can also be done through a record presentation of the lesson. The Step 2 (presentation) of an Intensive Reading lesson has no equivalent in Extensive Reading lessons. There is no model reading as part of an Extensive Reading

Lesson.

E. Teaching Composition

(a) **Speech techniques :** 1. Questioning by the teacher, 2. Inter-questioning by the pupils, 3. Repetition, 4. Conversion of tenses, pronouns and nouns.

(b) **Action techniques :** 1. Action completion on a thematic basis, 2. Dramatization of conversation, 3. Do and say for framing answers.

(c) **Picture techniques :** 1. Look and say, 2. Picture completion for story writing, 3. Development of a story by means of match-stick drawings.

F. Teaching Poetry

The presentation techniques for poetry would include the chief following techniques:

(a) **Model recitation** (Teacher's recitation),

(b) **Record presentation** (recitation from a recordplayer),

(c) **[illegible]c presentation** (recitation with dramatization),

(d) **[illegible] presentation** (recitation with a picture).

3. Te[illegible]es for Practice

A. Teaching Spoken English

DRILL

(a) **Speech techniques :** 1. Listen and say used when the pupils repeat with modification what the teacher speak; 2. Rote repetition (without any change), 3. Additive repetition (adds elements one by one. Also known as incremental repetition); 3. Variational repetition where the elements are changed while repeating; 4. Conversion repetition where phases and even clauses are changed while repeating. It can also be conversion from negative to positive, in tenses, voices etc.

(b) **Reading techniques :** 1. Flash cards for various types of repetition and sentence formation; 2 Read and say for patterns provided on the chalkboard or on flashcards; 3.

Nursery rhymes for practice of language material.

SITUATIONAL PRACTICE (Communicative Tasks)

(a) **Speech techniques :** 1. Look and say, 2. Questioning of situations, 3. Inter-questioning, 4. Group-tasks using the techniques mentioned.

(b) **Action technique :** 1. Do and say, 2. Read and do, 3. Listen and do, 4. Dramatization of several situations to use the speech item, 5. Dramatic recitation of rhymes, to use the particular speech-item; 6. Language games of several kinds: reading-games, speech-games, listening games; and writing games; 7. Extra-classroom experiences to make use of the speech forms; 8. Group-task where a few pupils undertake learning activities in class.

B. Teaching Structures

DRILL

(a) **Speech techniques :** 1. Listen and say for oral exercises using a particular pattern; 2. Rote repetition of a structure; 3. Additive (incremental) repetition, 4. Variational repetition by means of substitution tables; 5. Conversion repetition for a given pattern.

(b) **Reading techniques :** 1. Read and day using flash cards or the chalkboard; 2. Rote, additive, variational, and conversion repetitions using flashcards or the chalkboard.

SITUATIONAL PRACTICE (Communicative Tasks)

(a) **Speech techniques :** 1. Questioning on situations, 2. Inter-questioning, 3. Look and say for actions.

(b) **Action techniques :** 1. Do and say, 2. Listen and do, 3. Read and do, 4. Dramatization of several situations for the use of structure; 5. Dramatic recitation of nursery rhymes to use a structure; 6. Language games of several types : listening games, speech games, reading games, and writing games for the use of the structure; 7. Extra-classroom experiences by leading the pupils out into the school campus, shopping centres, post-office for practice in life situations; 8. Group-tasks for practice of the structure.

C. Teaching Vocabulary

DRILLS

(a) **Speech techniques :** 1. Listen and say for all types of exercise in which repetition is involved; 2. Pattern drill with additive, substitutional and conversional use of the newly learned word.

(b) **Reading techniques :** 1. Read and say exercise with additive, substitutional and conversion drills in which the new words are used; 2. Flash cards with the new words in different verbal contexts.

SITUATIONAL PRACTICE (Communicative Tasks)

(a) **Speech techniques :** 1. Questioning with the new words in a variety of situations; 2. Inter-questioning where the pupils learn to ask questions using the vocabulary items.

(b) **Action techniques :** 1. Do and say, 2. Listen and do for action words, 3. Dramatic recitation of nursery rhymes, 4. Language games using the new words; 5. Extra-classroom experiences, 6. Group-tasks using several of the techniques mentioned.

(c) **Reading techniques :** Read and say of paragraphs conversion, or rhymes where the new words are used. The teacher asks questions on the discourse. Inter-questioning possible.

D. Teaching Reading

Step 3 and 4 of an Intensive Reading lesson and Step 2 and 3 of an Extensive Reading lesson would require the following techniques : 1. Silent reading, 2. Silent reading after reading a set of questions for discussion; 3. Supervision by the teacher to take care of the 'mechanics' of reading; 4. Questioning, 5. Inter-questioning, 6. Group-work with a plenary session, and 7. Dramatization of the lesson where conversation is involved.

E. Teaching Composition

Step 3 of a composition lesson would require the following techniques; 1. Discourse-building orally or in writing, 2. Description of processes (past, present), features, characteristics, 3.

Biographical description 4. Narration of stories or events, 5. Conversation with stress on aspects of spoken English, 6. Conversion exercises of tense, persons, and situation. Conversion composition can also be both oral and written.

F. Teaching Poetry

Step 4 of a Poetry lesson would require the following techniques : 1. Questioning on the content, sound patterns, and language of the poem; 2. Inter-questioning, 3. Dramatic recitation, 4. Individual recitation, 5. Recitation supervision, 6. Group recitation, in various ways with close supervision by the teacher. Discussion can be in the form of group work with a concluding plenary session.

4. Techniques for Review

A. **Teaching Spoken English :** A variety of techniques have been recommended for the review part of an English lesson. At the same time there is a need to distinguish the Review part of a lesson (where ever there is one) from other Steps that we follow. The Review Step is meant to find out in a formal way how far and to what extent the lesson has been successful, and is to reflect the work of the pupils and, in turn, of the teacher. For these reasons it is found necessary that we make use of some objective test device to measure, as much as possible, what we exactly want to and only that aspect of the pupils' learning. Therefore the possibility to use a variety of techniques during the Review Step is ruled out. To review a Spoken lesson the following techniques can be used; 1. Read and say, 2. Listen and say, 3. Sentence formation, 4. Sentence completion.

B. **Teaching Grammar :** 1. Read and say in which the pupils make use of the exact structure in the exercises provided for the purpose and reveal if they have understood the meaning of the item and are able to use it in proper verbal context. This would include and exercise such as 1. Sentence completion, 2. Sentence formation, 3. Blank filling, 4. Multiple choice, 5. Matching items etc.

C. **Teaching Vocabulary :** Again, the objective of the Review Step of a Vocabulary lesson is to find out if the pupils have understood the meaning of the words and are able to use them in proper verbal contexts. The techniques are : 1. Read and say, 2. Bilingual matching, 3. Listen and say, 4. Sentence formation 5. Blank filling, and 6. Multiple choice.

D. Teaching Reading : The Review part of a Reading lesson would take care of two aspects of the pupils reading: (i) the reading speed, and (ii) comprehension. A measurement of the reading speech would require a word-count per minute, perhaps with the help of a stop-watch. But in normal circumstances the Review goes by way of testing only the pupil's comprehension. The techniques mentioned in *B and C* will be of great use in testing comprehension. It is also possible to test reading comprehension by getting the pupils answer questions in writing. But such full-fledged answers would bring the problem of *expression* when what we want is a testing only of the pupils' comprehension. Therefore to a great extent the need for measuring comprehension and the problems arising from expression are to be compromised at the time of test by making the test as specific and objective as possible.

5. Techniques for Remedial Work

A) Remedial Work for Spoken English

The present section takes care of only the teaching techniques that can be of use in remedial teaching of English. No remedial teaching is thought of for the teaching of English as a whole; such a programme is geared to the development of particular skills or areas of language *to fill the vacuum* left by a regular teaching programme. Therefore what is envisaged here is a skill-oriented remedial work to take care of all aspects of English language learning.

(1) ***Revision :*** Revision in a Remedial Programme for the teaching of spoken English would mean the revision of some specific language material in place of the usual *Presentation*. As the material is not new, no such presentation is required. The techniques to be used are : 1. Questioning with wherever possible the teacher himself answering the question ; 2. Look and say where the teacher does some activity

and the pupils verbalize it using the language material to be revised; 3. Listen and say which will consist of any oral exercise the teacher presents with the help of the pupils, *e.g.* additive repetition; 4. Miming where the teacher or a pupil imitates a character or an action and others verbalize the miming.

In the revision of *pronunciation* the teacher uses the listen and say technique in the sense of repetition.

(2) ***Drill :*** For purposes of drill in a remedial programme for spoken English see the techniques recommended under the *drill* part of the *Spoken English Lesson* (Sec. 3 of present Chapter)

(3) ***Situational Communicative Practice :*** Again to avoid repetition, the techniques recommended under Situational Practice (Sec. 3 of present Chapter) should be referred to for the same in remedial work.

(4) ***Review :*** The techniques included under the Review part of a Spoken English lesson (Sec. 4 of present Chapter) should be referred to.

B. Remedial Work in Grammar

(1) ***Revision :*** Just as in spoken English we deal with the *form*, *meaning* and *use* of some aspect of spoken English, in grammar too a remedial work would require revision in place of the usual presentation. The techniques to be used are the following:

(a) Questioning which if possible the teacher himself answers;

(b) Demonstration, not for making any meaning clear, but to obtain the verbal equivalents form the pupils. It will be a process of 'look and say' for the pupils.

(c) Listen and say is employed when any additive, substitutional or conversional exercises are involved, by means of which the structure is revised.

(2) ***Drill :*** The technique for drill in remedial teaching are the same as those recommended under the Drill Section of the present chapter (Sec.3.)

(3) ***Situational Practice :*** The techniques for situational practice are the same as those recommended under the situational practice of the present chapter (Sec. 3).

(4) ***Review :*** The techniques for Review in the remedial lesson for grammar are the same as those recommended under Review in Section 4.

C. Remedial Work in Vocabulary

(1) ***Revision :*** Along with various aspects of spoken English and grammar, work on vocabulary too is required. The revision vocabulary would be that of the relevant unit for remedial work. The following techniques can be used for revision: 1. Questioning to help the pupils to come out with sentences using the necessary vocabulary ; 2. Read and say exercises to help the pupils use the words in patterns ; 3. Listen and say technique for framing various kinds of sentences orally; 4. Verbal illustration to bring home the meaning of doubtful vocabulary items; 5. Bilingual presentation to teach the meaning of very difficult words.

(2) ***Drill :*** The techniques for drill are the same as those given in Section 3 of the present chapter.

(3) ***Situational :*** The techniques for situational practice are the same as those given in Section 3 of the present chapter.

(4) ***Review :*** Again, the techniques given in Section 4 are relevant to the review work in a remedial lesson.

D. Remedial Work in Reading

Reading should form part of the remedial teaching in schools. The techniques and the procedures are the same as those recommended for the regular lesson in intensive and extensive reading.

E. Remedial Work in Composition

Any remedial work on a unit should end with composition. The teaching of remedial composition will follow the same techniques as those recommended for regular Oral and Written Composition (see Ch. 11 of 'Teaching English in India' for details).

11
Teaching English in Universities

1. The Need for Substantial Reforms

University education in our country has always been subjected to severe criticism due to its conspicuous inability to cope with the growing academic requirements of the country. The chief reason for this being the irrelevance of the university courses to the needs of contemporary India. This aspect is much more true of the present English teaching in our universities and college, then anything else. An analysis of the present situation would point to the following problems :

(1) English courses in our universities and colleges both at the graduate and undergraduate levels are literature-oriented. Today English in our universities is more or less identified with literature. The English syllabuses in our universities are overloaded with literature. All would agree that there is nothing wrong with teaching literature. It would also be almost impossible to visualize an English course at a graduate or post-graduate level without having some recourse to English literature. Literature is the aesthetic, artistic and immensely creative use of language and it introduces the life-pulses of a society in some genre or other. One would not certainly minimise the role of literature in English teaching.

But this is not the whole of the problem. In a country

like ours where English functions mostly at the level of L_2 and L_3, and where our school have certainly failed to impart the basic skills of English language, a continued emphasis on something other than actual down-to-earth language teaching would be futile. This is indeed, a widely accepted fact. What the Indian universities need as we shall examine later, is a language-oriented course with a view to equipping our students for various language requirements in their professional life. Instead today our students coming out of the universities have neither language nor literature, the latter without the former being something difficult to visualize.

(2) Another stumbling book to a proper English language course in Indian universities is the widely held belief that even the teaching of literature cannot be thought of without introducing the student to Old and Middle English literature. One certainly doubts the relevance and utility of these aspects of early English literature in a context where the average Indian student is strikingly in need of introduction to English language itself and to the present-day literature. Irrespective of the Southern or Northern universities only a very small percentage of our students are in a position to express themselves in spoken English, to understand a standard work or to write an essay in feasibily good English. Teaching any irrelevant material such as Old or Middle English and the literature of the period is certainly of no use.

(3) Although there are several such features which may be discussed here, one that certainly requires attention is the teacher-problem. How many of the teachers in our universities and colleges have gone beyond their M.A., or M.Sc., or any other pre-doctoral degree ? As almost all States today sponsor in service-course such as summer institutes for college and university teachers, at least a few take the benefit of these opportunities. This is only one aspect of the teacher-problem. There are two essential qualities a university teacher should possess: Considerable acquaintence with the specialised subject and the ability to convey this knowledge. It is difficult to identify, as some tend to do, a university teacher with a *research scholar*. All research

scholars do not make essentially successful university teachers. In other words knowledge in the subject, proficiency in the language functioning as the medium, and the skill to convey this knowledge one way or other to the students are essential qualities of a teacher in a university or a college. It is a deplorable fact that our universities house dumb and deaf research scholars or block-headed chatter-boxes. Either of these categories fail to function as teachers capable of commanding the student's attention, interest and enthusiasm in the teaching-learning process.

(4) Another problem crucial enough in this context is that of the teaching methods. The author certainly does not advocate that all university teachers must have their B.Ed. degree. But there are several ways by which teachers in universities and colleges may be introduced to a variety of teaching methods which will prove extremely useful in teaching situations. Today the college teacher is hardly aware of anything but lecturing to the class. Certainly lecture has its big role to play in teaching in universities. There are instance where no other method can effectively replace lectures. In the following pages we shall take up the discussion as to what methods and teaching techniques can be followed by the university teacher.

Although one may not recommend making B.Ed., compulsory to teachers in this context, it would be very much advisable to recruit to universities and colleges teachers who along with their post-graduate qualifications possess a bachelor's degree in teaching. It will be very misleading to consider degrees in teaching a requisite only to those working in schools or colleges of education. A snobbish attitude towards this requirement on the part of the university teacher is certainly deplorable.

2. The New Role of Universities

Against this background we may rightly assume that the Indian universities have altogether a new role to play to solve the manifold problems that have arisen from the lack of adequate education. Here too as in the foregoing section we may examine the situations in a systematic manner:

(1) The universities are no longer the custodians of mere higher education only, alienated from the practical requirements and problems of the country. So far the teaching of English was dealt with in two different ways, as we have been seeing in the foregoing chapters: (i) imparting the basic skills of the language, and (ii) imparting the knowledge or information about the deeper aspects of English language including its use in literature. The former has been considered the business of schools and the latter that of the university. Schools were expected to teach the children how to speak read and write English while the universities were expected to teach the literature, linguistics and the history of English.

This seems to be a fine way of doing things and it is bound to be a success where conditions are feasible. But in our country today, schools are not in a position to produce students who are conversant with the language. Very small per cent of the aspirants to colleges and universities today have achieved any significant level of proficiency in the English language skills that enable them to face the requirements of the higher education successfully. Several factors have contributed to this predicament which we are not in a position to discuss here. As a consequence the universities can no longer rightly claim to be the custodians of only the higher levels of education because such a thing do not mean anything in the present context. The universities cannot talk of x, y, z, when the very a, b, c, is missing. This is a major challenge which our universities have to take up. The inadequate education the schools are imparting should somehow be made up at the university level and establish the missing link between the two stages of education. This problem is most acute in the area of *English language teaching*. This is major reason for our emphasis to reform the courses and syllabuses followed in our universities.

(2) Another aspect which needs consideration is the present-day requirements of English for *special purposes*. Much noise is made about ESP and its necessity but so far hardly anything is done by way of benefit to the students. The present-day 'groping-in-the-dark type' of English courses take us no where closer to the target of equipping the

students technically or professionally. Ours is a set of courses like the procrustean bed on to which the individual is fastened and cut to shape. How long can we go on with English courses of this kind? Therefore the way out is to reorganize our syllabuses and courses in such a way as to bring in specialised areas of English and thus meet the student's requirement when he is out in the word in a specific profession. In otherwords, the English for which a student spends over five years must be of some practical utility to him in the context of his profession. This is where the urgent need for some sort of bifurcated English course arises.

(3) Indian universities today have another major role to play in increasing and further consolidating the status of English. The universities more and more to shift over to the regional language as the medium of instruction. It's certainly a tragic situation. The universities which are supposed to be the custodians and promoters of whatever English still India can have, themselves decry its use. The report of the Education Commission may be remembered in this context when it said, 'English will continue to enjoy a high status so long as it remains the principal medium of education at the university stage, and the language of administration at the centre and in many of the States. Even after the regional languages becomes media in higher education a working knowledge of English will be valuable asset for all students and reasonable proficiency in the language will be necessary for those who proceed to the university.' What the Education Commission envisaged as 'the principal medium of education at the university' is already but of question in most of our universities today. Even at places where the official medium is English, the actual work goes on in the regional language.

At least what the Commission called 'a working knowledge' of English sounds a reasonable target for every educated Indian. To achieve at least this objective, departments of English in colleges and universities must work with a new awareness of the need. In otherwords, a lot can be done by our English departments by way of regular *departmental work* and by means of *extension services* to radiate an English environment in the entire university and in the region, provided this awareness of the need is powerfully followed up. We shall examine some of the ways out in the following pages. There should not be even one chance in a hundred to use the regional language in the teaching of English in universities. Once even the departments of English permit the loophole what right have we to expect other departments to teach especially the social sciences in the medium of English? In the following pages we shall be examining a few concrete way of assuming these new roles in the reaching of English and what methods and techniques could be employed in the teaching of English in universities. Chalking out a comprehensive plan is beyond the scope of this section, but a few concrete proposals would certainly of use to improve the situation.

3. Methods of Teaching English in Universities

Although most teachers in universities are conversant with a variety of teaching techniques, very few in fact take pains to employ them effectively in the classroom. Techniques are implementational devices, a variety of which alone can make teaching varied and interesting. Teaching English in universities may be seen as a unified activity consisting of several sub-components, both at the graduate and post-graduate levels : 1. *Prose*, 2. *Poetry*, 3. *Criticism*, 4. *Linguistics* (Phonology, Morphology, Syntax, and Semantics), 5. *History of English Language*, 6. *Spoken English*, 7. *Reading*, 8. *Writing*.

(1) The Teaching of Prose : It has been customary to treat prose, poetry, criticism and language in the same manner, employing exclusively the lecture method and mostly rendering the students passive listeners and in-takers. The present-day requirements call for innovative measures in teaching the subjects mentioned above, a more active participation by the students in the teaching-learning experiences, and a feeling that each one is wanted in the classroom to make teaching-learning a more satisfactory experience. The following methods may be employed in teaching prose (drama, fiction, essays) in universities:

(a) *Lecture*: The essential role the lecture method plays in university teaching cannot be overlooked. Whatever be the inadequacy, lecture method of teaching stands as the most basic teaching method in the context of university education. But most people have the misconception that lecture means a one-way-recourse and that the teacher is supposed to be doing all the talking and that too in high momentum. Lecture needs to be supplemented with several other techniques to make it most fruitful and effective. Intermittent *questioning* should become an essential part of lecturing. Two kinds of questions may be asked : *reflective* as well as *genuine* questions. The teacher amidst speaking stops and poses certain questions with a view to helping the pupils think further on important points. No answer is expected here, the purpose is merely to elicit interest and mentally attempt answers. Genuine questioning expects answers from the students. The questions need to be short, lucid, and easy so that they do not become a test of the student's brilliance or of the teacher's exuberance. These questions can be based on the material immediately presented or on points that the teacher intends to present later. In either way questions serve several purposes : (i) questioning keeps the students all the more alert and holds their attention; (ii) questioning links various aspects of the lecture and enables the students to keep trace of an view the lecture in a unified manner; (iii) questioning functions as a revision technique amidst a lecture and helps the students to consolidate and remember the teaching material; and lastly, (iv) questioning adds interest and variety to teaching and helps the students to genuinely participate in the teaching-learning process.

Teacher is universities fight shy of questioning due to several reasons. It is said to be a major source of interruption to the continuous flow of lecture. The answer can be simple that no such 'fire-brand' lecture needs to be a part of university teaching. The teacher must train himself to be continually interrupted to make the lecture more fruitful to the students. This is true especially in a situation where the students possess no mastery over the language of the medium.

Apart from questioning being made an integral aspect of lectures, there are a few other techniques which add colour to a good lecture. For several teachers the chalkboard is an anathema during lectures. Again, the *chalkboard* serves a number of effective purposes during lectures : (i) first of all, a lecture provides only an audio-lingual modality for the students to cling on. Occasional jottings, illustrations, presentations of difficult names and words, and central points of the lecture provide additional modality for stimuli and help the students' comprehension of the teaching point; (ii) the chalkboard in a special way helps the slow-learner in tracing the lecture points and in taking down notes at his own speed; (iii) the chalkboard helps teachers organize the teaching material and flash back on to points that need to be referred to. The university teacher may never fight shy of the chalkboard presuming that the chalkboard is the school teachers' teaching aid. From the primary to post-graduate levels the chalkboard has specific roles to play in making teaching effective.

Lectures may be made effective by provision of the lecture points in the class in advance. This may be done through mimeographed sheets. The lecture-points certainly make the lecture more concrete, easily accessible and feasible enough to remember and elaborate them later at convenient time. These points, again, one of the great helps to the teacher as he is in a position to remember and organize his material. Finally, lectures need to be supplemented with a set of question which the students are required to answer at home. These questions certainly help them prepare themselves better for tests and examinations. Lecture in universities are bound to be successful if they are made more effective through a few other techniques as recommended above.

(b) ***Tutorial Method :*** Tutorial is a much misused and misinterpreted method of teaching in universities. In the name of tutorials a lecture class is divided into groups and the teacher-in-charge turns the same into a mini-lecture class, with little or no participation by the students. But the tutorial is highly potential to generate good discussion on a relevant topic and obtain practice in the use of the language skills and to broaden the pupils' view on a particular subject. Tutorial classes are meant primarily for student participation through discussion. For this purpose the tutorial classes are kept as small as they could be. The number very much depends, in practical situations, on the availability of teachers for the purpose. The student-teacher ratio is not satisfactory. The problem of large number does not arise in our post-graduate departments as the number of students is always small.

An effective conducting of the tutorial classes requires that the teachers come prepared for this specific purpose. The best way is to get prepared with set of question on a specific topic. The teacher in the tutorial class is only a guide. To ensure effective work the material to be discussed should be as much as from topics covered in the regular lecture class. A tutorial is a kind of follow-up work. The questions are given to the class; the students take up the questions, one by one, and attempt to arrive at the most adequate answers. The teacher's contribution requires to be the least. The students should strive the way up, discuss the answers, get the mistakes corrected and ensure correct answers to the questions. The teacher has to make sure that the maximum number of students participate in the discussion, and that no set of individuals unduly dominate the discussion.

Any one students capable of taking down notes may be asked to keep trace of the discussion. At the end of the discussion he will present the answers to all the questions as discussed in the group. This will enable the students to have an overall view of the answers and if needed write down for themselves. The use of tutorial classes for developing the language skills may be discussed in the following pages. The success of the tutorial classes very much depends on the teachers themselves. The excuse that the students have no language proficiency to answer questions and take part in discussions cannot be entertained. The tutorials are meant to overcome all these defects to a large extent. The embarrassment of speaking English in a large class may be avoided in such small groups where the students must feel free. Continuous encouragement and persuation will certainly enable our university students to participate in and contribute towards better discussion and use of the language. The tutorial classes are certainly the best to achieve individual student participation.

(c) ***Seminar Method :*** One of the principal aims of university education is to help the student achieve a high level of independence with regard to study habits and inculcate the habit of personal study. The post-graduate student especially cannot afford to neglect the essential role personal studies and research habits are going to play in his professional life. He must be aptly equipped for the purpose. Seminars as practised today in our universities have hardly any noble aim to cherish. Seminars, like tutorials have become almost ritualistic and they are a stumbling block to the easy-going university routine.

Seminars have very clear-cut things to achieve. Unlike tutorials, seminar groups may be larger. In graduate classes with a large number of students present, it is advisable to form smaller groups. The divisions into smaller groups enables a greater number of eager students to participate in the seminar. It is most unwise to distribute the topics for the seminar just a weak or so in advance. It is possible for any department or individual teacher to plan out the year's work and get ready with a list of topics in the beginning of the academic year, and make it available to all the students. The advantages are many. As the essential feature of a seminar is to present a paper two with follow-up discussions among the students, the individuals responsible for a topic may have it at his disposal quite in advance. It will also save any last minute hurry to find out a suitable topic for the papers.

A student or two prepare a paper on the specific topic allocated for the purpose. The papers are presented before the class or the group. The guiding teacher should be present in order to help a better presentation of the paper and the follow-up discussion. As it happens, the concentration may not be exclusively on the content matter of the paper. It is of equal importance to focus attention on the aspects of presentation and the language of the paper. Seminars are not merely to enhance scholarship, but to develop the communicative proficiency of the student, an aspect which may be demanded of him in any profession than the scholarship he may have achieved.

The organization and the level of standard of the essay including aspects of usage must be taken care of. Exceptionally clever students fail to perform well in examinations and in occasions such as seminars due to their inability to organize their material and present it in a acceptable manner. The same ability is required of a university teacher to organize and present one's material before the students in a scheduled time so as to be beneficial to the students.

Seminar should not be allocated on a voluntary basis. Every student may be in a position to do his best in reading a paper. The principal motivation that may be provided to boost interest in students is to include seminars as a part of the assessment. It is an encouraging this that several universities do this. Again, the success of all these attempts lies in with what sincerely and genuine interest the teacher and the students take up the seminars. Ultimately all success in education depends on the learner's dedicated work. The teacher and the methods are all of secondary importance.

(d) ***Arm-chair Method:*** We may employ the term for one of the most effective teaching methods in university education. Some of the basic principles of effective education have been applied here. The requirements for :(i) the smallest number, (ii) personal liaison, (iii) relaxed atmosphere for intellectual work, (iv) facility for immediate and on-the-spot clarification and help, and (v) on-the-spot testing are all met in a method of this kind. It is better advisable for a teacher to meet a group of students profitably twice a week than to meet them every day for a lecture that invariably goes overhead. It is equally advisable to work thoroughly on a few novels or plays rather than rush through a dozen of them, reading them in class rather than asking on students to read them at home.

The arm-chair method suggested in the present work consists of the following: we have a teacher and a group of students consisting not more than ten. The classroom needs be specially arranged as it is usually done for seminars. It means that the entire work is done in a feasibly set and psychologically favourable atmosphere. The teacher is not on the lecture-platform; he relaxes with the students. The students are not seated upright on the traditional benches; they relax in their comfortable chairs. All feel very much at home; the atmosphere counts much in bringing home learning. At least a few good reference books are readily available at hand. If this class is held in the departmental library, it is all the better.

The moment the teacher is down from his 'platform' the intensity of his lecture decreases. He has to speak to them now; there is more of conversational atmosphere in the classroom. The students are free to ask questions, take part in the discussion even in their limpid language. They are no longer afraid of standing up and speaking in an awesome atmosphere. The teacher speaks to them, asks questions as suggested in the lecture method, answers the student's querries, explains things, always ready to stop and listen to the students. Completion of a particular teaching point is not his concern; he endeavours to lead the students to the proper insight into the material. The students have enough time to take down points. The teacher has time to think and organize his material as well as to do justice to those new insights that dawn on him. His controlled fluency permits them to interrupt any moment they wish and clear things.

One of the major advantages of the present method is that the teacher can have easy testing on the spot. The principle of continuous testing is well applicable here. Any moment he may turn on the students and ask for clarification. The level of attention and the level of achievement may easily be found out. As the teacher is in close, personal contact with the students, there is practically nothing that hinders them from taking active participation in the teaching-learning experiences.

Again, if the arm-chair method fails, it may not be due

to its own inadequacy, but the influence of those factors which usually render any method futile; lack of interest in tapping the best resource on the part of the teacher and the students. In normal circumstances where it is feasible to have such a small group and the facilities needed to make the meet congenial, the arm-chair method may prove to be perhaps one of the few competent methods of teaching in universities.

(e) ***Assignment Method:*** Teaching through assignments have been widely accepted as a way of getting some substantial work done by students especially at the post-graduate level. But the fact that ready-made assignments are available to any one on the lookout for them brings down the utility of the assignment method. Assignments have only a supplementary value; this method may not substitute the work done in class. Taken genuinely on both the ends, teachers and students, the method of assignments is fundamentally very valuable in university education.

Assignments and seminars could be combined wherever possible Combining these two will make the students work on the paper even if they happen to have borrowed it from elsewhere. Once the seminar-reading has been done the paper could be accepted as the individuals's assignment. Wherever this is not possible something must be done to ensure that the student has a share in preparing the assignment. Assignments help the students read related books. This is one of the chief objectives of this method A Simple essay prepared by them should be preferred to bulk of material duplicated from a source-book. Every student may be required to submit a fixed number of assignments in course of the academic year. But the relevance of these assignments to the particular course must be carefully ensured.

(2) ***Teaching Poetry :*** It is difficult to earmark the kind of specific methodology required for teaching poetry in universities. There is a fundamental difference between teaching poetry in schools and in universities. The objectives vary greatly. We have at length discussed the problem of teaching poetry in schools. Poetry is taught in school with a view to

developing the skill of appreciation. Language has an aesthetic side; language is employed for aesthetic, artistic purposes. Poetry consists in the artistic use of language with its creative potentials stretched to the maximum and with emphasis on the employment of sound patterns such as rhythm, rhyme etc. If we create an environment in which the pupils apply their faculty for appreciation and enjoy the organization of language, we may rightly say that the aim of teaching poetry in schools is fulfilled.

It is with a higher purpose that poetry is included in the university English syllabus. University education intends to develop and sharpen the student's critical faculty. The sense of critical appreciation and critical judgement is evoked in the teaching of poetry. The college student may be in a position to appreciate the thematic content and the employment of language, and at the same time see critically the worth of the material that is before him. Thus teaching poetry in universities should serve a double purpose : on the one hand what we try to do in schools is continued, and on the other personal role is assumed. The teacher enables the students to think in tune with the posts of the ages; and he helps the student pick and choose worthwhile material and worthwhile content. The faculties of imagination and intellect are on the one hand satisfied with the poet's imaginative and intellectual presentation of a phenomenon, while on the other the faculty of the will picks and chooses aspects of personal appeal *i.e.* things that are appealing to the student himself. Here in lies the critical role of teaching poetry. It is not merely branding something as good or bad. It is some kind of a personal identification and the acute ability to achieve it. The teacher in the university must aim at developing and sharpening this potentiality or faculty for personal identification with worthwhile experiences presented by the poet in worthwhile organization of language.

As we aim at achieving all these in the teaching of poetry, the teacher, endeavouring to attack all the three faculties : the *imagination*, the *intellect*, and the *will*, is required to be in very close contact with the student-body. The *arm-chair method* recommended above seems to be the most suited method for the teaching of poetry.

(4) The Teaching of Criticism

It may be observed that all teaching of criticism in universities is a teaching of the history of criticism; therefore it hardly differs from the teaching of any other aspects of prose or history. Again, if criticism is meant to introduce the graduate or post-graduate students to the texture of the principles of criticism, then it cannot be treated as simple prose. One of the major objectives here too should be to inculcate in the students to study a text, a play, a poem, or any work with a scientific bent of mind and to move his critical faculty on the quality of the material from all aspects necessary. It may not happen that the post-graduate student enters the classroom, listens to a series of lectures as usual which make no difference to him, and leaves with a few jottings as in different as he could be. Criticism should be a much more personal things and with it should go a sense of responsibility. Which ever of the methods recommended above we may use, the students should have the feeling that they are doing something noble, that they are trying too look into something which they themselves are not in a position to understand fully, not to speak of producing it. Instead of fully concentrating on the history of criticism, the students may have access to some level of original critical attempts.

(5) The Teaching of Language Skills

The aspects discussed above are mostly pertaining to things already included in today's university curriculum. What is incredibly lacking is the teaching of language skills. It today's schools have failed to achieve their targets in language teaching, then in order to save future of English in our country, the university departments in charge of English cannot neglect the teaching of the basic language skills. If not, ours will be a mansion built on shifting sands. The English syllabus of our universities should include the teaching of speaking, reading, and writing for purposes of developing these skills.

(a) ***Teaching Spoken English:*** All that needs be said about the importance of language skills, the differences among them, their specific roles etc. have been covered in the foregoing chapters on the foundations of methodology. By the time a student is in a college or a university, a major portion of his English language formation gets completed. The teacher in the university has to assume additional responsibilities in-order to help the students achieve proficiency in spoken English. Without sparing any regular lecture period, a fair number of tutorials can be used for this purpose. Most of the techniques recommended in the chapter on Spoken English could be employed in teaching spoken English in the university. The following may be a few specific methods used:

(i) In the tutorial class questions on a specific grammatical item may be used to elicit answers from the students. A well-prepared syllabus of language items could work as the basis for it.

(ii) The use of oral composition will work wonders in teaching spoken English. The teacher with the help of the response from the students develop a set of points on a topic. After having a set of points on the blackboard, each student may be asked to work out a whole paragraph on the topic. These paragraphs may be descriptive, narrative or explanatory.

(iii) Work can be done on a dialogue: the students can very well work out a dialogue on an interesting topic. This may be related to something they have on the syllabus: a play, novel etc. Dramatizing a scene from relevant play, in simple language, can serve the purpose.

(iv) A very fruitful way of providing practice in spoken English is to have either ex-tempore or prepared speech-sessions. Unlike in schools this is very well possible in university classes. Under the teacher's guidance, the students should speak freely on a topic. Corrections should be made on the spot on all aspects of presentation as the chief purpose there is the development of proficiency. The teacher's imagination is the best source in finding out ways of providing practice in spoken English.

(b) The Teaching of Reading : As it has been visualized, the day is not far off when English will serve Indians chiefly

as a library language. Even if this is not going to be the case, English is the major library language for the educated and for the post-graduate students in our universities. But the level of reading efficiency *i.e.* the reading speed and the comprehension exercised by students is, perhaps, the minimum. A book in technical language is still a stumbling block to our students. The difficulty in reading from the viewpoints of speed and comprehension may be the major reason for even the post-graduate students neglecting reading.

Amidst the packed schedule of the university if some time may be found for teaching reading, it will prove very fruitful. Since it is not possible for a university teacher to remain with a set of students busy reading for thirty minutes, a way out could be recommended. A particular section should be earmarked for reading; the students can read the section at home. The teacher is ready with a set of questions (objective type) and the day after the test is administered to the class. It may not be possible to do well in the test unless the student takes pains to read through the material. If this is repeated with some regular material for study, such reading will prove most useful.

(c) ***The Teaching of Writing:*** The exercises mentioned above regarding the teaching of reading skill will prove most useful in writing too. It is fine way of combining both reading and writing, and of getting something written for the teacher's assessment. In spite of all that we may speak of the difference between guided and free compositions and essays, even the present-day university student very much needs guidance in writing an essay of any standard. The language, the content and the organization of the content require constant control by the teacher to be effective. A free-style essay is almost out of question.

Unlike reading, the teacher cannot depend on any material the students bring written from home. Consequently some time may be found for getting paragraphs or short assignments worked out in the class. The tutorial classes, again, can serve this purpose. Even if it is time consuming, and cannot be done frequently, the teacher may find some time to do the corrections and return the material. Teaching written English alone can equip our university students to do well in their examinations as per the present system. A professional life from all aspects requires that the students going out of the universities should be able to cope with the language problem.

The future of English in our country depends much on how the Indian universities equip themselves in attacking the problem whatever may be shifting policies of politicians. Keeping aside the pertinent differences of opinion with regard to the role of English in higher education, the co-ordinated efforts should be to see that English does not turn out to be merely a language of the elite for reading or reference purposes. If English must be kept alive in the country, the language skills should invariably be in the focus in English teaching in universities. Whether it be the teaching of prose, poetry, criticism or history, apart from the communication and consolidation of the pertinent information, the co-ordinate aim should be enable the students to use the language proficiently. It is a matter of simple commonsense that proficiency in the language of the medium should be preferred to a bulk of information in the literature of the language in the context of university education. Ability to express oneself on an Indian author should be preferred to the knowledge of Chaucer, Milton or Shakespeare. What naturally comes first should receive priority. Only a conscientious effort to equip our university students of English with reasonable proficiency will solve the problems English teaching in our universities is facing today.

12
Teaching English in English Medium Schools

1. Attitude Towards Methodology

English medium schools and L_1 schools meet very different problems in regard to the teaching of English. As we have seen in connection with the discussion of the difference between English as L_1 and English as L_2 (Ch. 2), Indian children, for instance, learn English in very different circumstances. In urban homes where English is spoken for one or two generations English happens to be the first language that the child picks up. There are children who learn English before the school-going age from neighbours who speak English at home.

English medium schools have these and other categories of pupils such as those who learn English purely as a second language. In otherwords the English medium school-going pupils can be very well grouped into (i) those who enter formal schooling with fairly good mastery of or at least introduction to English language, and (ii) those who join school without any knowledge of English at all and for whom English is strictly a second language. The first group consists of two sub-groups : (a) those who have the opportunity to use English at home like any L_1 learner, and (b) those who use English along with another language which is said to be the child's mother-tongue.

For these reasons, English-medium schools face certain peculiar problems. The groups available in any English medium schools are more heterogenous than those found in L_1 schools. There are those who speak only English at home and those who speak only the mother-tongue at home. Between these two extremes there are a variety of backgrounds from which pupils come so far as language is concerned. It is such a compelling heterogeneity that a teacher in an English-medium school faces. In these circumstances there are several methodological factors with which the teacher as to come to compromise. What methodology should the teacher employ to teach English in such circumstances. Teachers in India are trained to teach English exclusively as a foreign (second) language. Seldom is any training focussed on the sort of pupils who learn English only within the four walls of the classroom. Consequently a fresh teacher of English uses a set of methods of teaching English in group of pupils who have obtained fair mastery over the language before they join school, a set of methods which is meant to teach English only as a second language that the pupils for the first time learn in the classroom. This is in fact is the gist of the problem that the teacher of English faces in an English-medium school.

For these reasons, teachers in English-medium schools take great liberty in regard to the methods of teaching English. In the last resort it comes to be that no formal and specific method is required to teach English in such schools. The teacher due to the inadequacy of the existing set of methods and teaching techniques to meet the marked heterogeneity of classes mostly takes resort to one and only method of explanation of teaching items and formal grammar teaching. The teacher has mostly one method to teach any aspect of a teaching unit: formal explanation of everything. Teaching *grammar* consists of explanation of the relevant aspects of grammar (say, parts of speech), explanation of the definitions, rules and their exceptions, and a great deal of written experiences for practice. Teaching *vocabulary* would consist of providing known English equivalents with some illustrative sentences for greater clarification. Teaching *reading* would boil down to reading aloud by the teacher before the explanation and subsequent reading aloud by the pupils. The teaching of a *lesson* in the textbook is something separate from grammar, which is treated by means of outright explanatory discussion solely by the teacher. The great variety of teaching techniques which are at the disposal of the teacher of English to make teaching effective and interesting are seldom made use of. All that happens in the classroom is that the teacher takes a great deal and the pupils listen. Composition is again a silent and lonely endeavour on the part of the pupils, and the teacher is expected only to make corrections later. No distinction to made between oral and written compositions. Poetry is, again, taught by means of formal explanation of the thematic content and the language used. In otherwords teaching English in English-medium school is mostly the teacher's work of formal explanation, and the pupil's work of writing. These two would make the sum total of the teaching methodology in English-mediums schools except when very brilliant and enthusiastic teachers introduce any other techniques in the classroom.

There are few teachers who make a formal distinction among the various *types of lessons* mentions above. The lesson in the textbook is dealt with as if a unit depending only on its length, which will be divided into two or three portions for teaching purposes. The lesson is seldom viewed as a unit which consists of several parallel aspects such as the structures, vocabulary, text for reading, which finally lead to discourse building in the form of oral or written composition. As a result the teacher of English does not find it necessary to co-ordinate a series of sub-units (aspects of the lesson) under the unit which we call a lesson in the textbook. The teacher outright begins dealing with the lesson in the textbook and dedicates a few classes at random for its completion by means of formal explanations and written exercises until the lesson is completed.

In fact, there is a slack attitude towards methodology in English-medium schools. Despite repeated efforts by enlightened principals and educationists to fill the vacuum of proper methodology in English-medium schools, it happens that perhaps due to the force of circumstances even well-trained and resourceful teachers of English fail to organize classroom teaching by means of effective teaching techniques recommended for the purpose. This slack attitude towards methodology adversely affects the latter group of pupils in English-medium schools, who have little or no English *language atmosphere* at home, and who depend in turn entirely on classroom teaching for learning English. The English language atmosphere readily available in most English-medium schools is the most advantageous factor so far as learning is concerned. It is the most *desired condition* required for the proper acquisition of English. The coupled with proper methods of teaching English at all levels would certainly render English teaching effective beyond doubts.

2. Language Atmosphere of English-medium Schools

It is seen that the greatest asset of English-medium schools is the English atmosphere readily available for pupils of any level to listen to and speak the language the way required. An English-medium school possesses English atmosphere for several reasons. First of all, a good percentage of students come from English speaking families where from a very early age they get acquainted with the language. These pupils certainly take the lead in using English in the school, both in and outside the classroom. Their command over the language and enthusiasm in using the language function as a great motivating factor for others to pick up the language much sooner than expected. Secondly, unlike schools where the L_1 is the medium, English-medium schools have the subjects taught through the medium of English. However adequately this may be done now-a-days in most cities of the country, it still provides tremendous potential for the pupils to acquire command over the language. Thirdly, English-medium schools are mostly situated in towns and cities. This urban atmosphere helps the pupils come across people in the community, who speak English for a variety of purposes. Similarly, metropolitan or cosmopolitan cities have a variety of communal situations such as shops, post-offices, restaurants etc. where English is often heard spoken. The upper class as well as the upper middle class in our cities and towns have plenty of opportunity to listen to and speak English outside their homes and schools provided such situations are somehow utilized.

Such language atmosphere has a lot to do with the proficiency the pupils obtain although much depend on the learning experiences provided in the classroom. Greatest *language proficiency* may be expected of those pupils who have English atmosphere, in the classroom, in the school, at home, and out in the community. The least language proficiency may be expected of those pupils who have no opportunity to listen to and use good English even in the classroom. Between these two extremes, again, there are a variety of types depending on the sort of atmosphere available to use English. It has been more and more accepted that effective language learning takes place only if the language comes to be used in meaningful life situations (Ch. 11). English used in the classroom, in the school, at home and in the community meet such a requirement in all it dimensions, and depending on what level of language atmosphere is absent the effectiveness of learning is adversely affected.

3. Methods of Teaching in English-medium Schools

The resourceful English atmosphere of English-medium schools coupled with effective *teaching methodology* will certainly yield significant fruits as far as learning English is concerned. What is required primarily is departure from the usual practice of formal explanation and exercises in writing, and an approach that would distinguish a teaching unit as a complex of several elements and aspects which require separate treatment for practical purposes. *Lesson 5* in the textbook of Std. X, for instance, is not simple but a complex teaching unit which require differentiated treatment as has been developed in course of the preceding chapters.

It is true that a strictly *graded approach* to language teaching is relevant only to the teaching of English in schools where L_1 is the medium. At the same time it must be remembered that no formal (by contrast to informal) teaching of English can be undertaken without bringing in some level of graded organization of language material. Again, a strictly functional teaching of English for the development of the language skills may not be required in the case of those for whom English is almost the L_1 (group 1 mentioned in Sec. 1), but today's vast majority in English-medium schools do require some kind of a functional teaching of the language for them to reach the expected level of mastery over the language. Students from the L_1 background are yet to obtain command over the aural-oral (listening-speaking) skills of English, and the primary purpose of any course in English is the same while students from an English background with a fair command over the language may not require a strictly functional and skill-oriented teaching of English. While a strictly skill-oriented teaching of English would be required for groups (ii) as done in L_1 schools, the requirements of groups (i) call for a mixed approach which takes care of both *formal* and *functional* teaching of language items.

In certain cases it is recommended that a separation be made between group (i) and group (ii) for purposes of effective teaching. But such a separate grouping on the basis of language proficiency may not help solve the problems of group (ii). Better justice may be done to group (ii) in the context of an English-medium school if it is give the gull opportunity to take advantage of the language proficiency of group (i). Allowing a congenial condition for group (ii) to sit with group (i) and take advantage of the proficiency of group (i) would be the best solution to the problems of group (ii). In otherwords, the teacher of English needs to bear in mind the requirements of both the groups and as such as possible order his classroom teaching techniques accordingly so as to meet these distinct requirements. The following methodology is recommended for teaching English in English-medium schools.

(a) ***The Teaching of Grammar:*** English medium schools still entertain, queer notions regarding the teaching of English grammar. Grammar teaching is seldom properly related to the textbook, the workbook or composition. In many schools not even the same teacher teach grammar and the textbook. Teaching grammar still follows the traditional pattern of adhering to a grammar book of the old type. Definitions, rules and exceptions predominate, and there is still place for much committing to memory. Only at the level of resourceful individual teachers has some *functional work* introduced alongwith the learning of *formal grammar*.

There is simply no justification even at the upper primary levels of an English medium school to teach the formal theoretical aspects of grammar. The formal, theoretical treatment of English grammar should begin only from the high school classes, while under present circumstances in L_1 schools formal, theoretical treatment of English grammar is not required at all even at the high school level, expect acquainting the high school students with the basic and essential grammatical terminology for their information and subsequent recognition of structures.

At the lower and upper primary levels of the English medium school the teacher will concentrate on the structures of English from a functional point of recommended above. This would mean *closely relating the textbook* lessons with all other aspects of English the teacher is expected to handle. The lesson in the textbook is considered the unit from which all other works emerge. The lesson is not a mere aid to teaching, but a resourceful starting point and its compressed characteristic provides the teacher with ample material to work. A skill-oriented teaching of English will prove most useful in English medium schools because of the presence of English atmosphere.

Structural approach and direct (listening-speaking) method would prove so much so that the pupils in English medium schools with their language background would pick up the structures and correct usage with starting speed. An the lower and upper primary levels no distinction need be made between formal and functional teaching of grammar. What the teacher should aim at is to help the pupils obtain greater command over the structures of English and modern usage, instead of attempting to give him information about English grammar. *Graded structures* will be capable of rationalizing the pupils' knowledge of the language. In the case of the former group (i) which possesses English background the teacher's work can be considered in line with the following points : (i) rationalizing and systematizing the pupils' knowledge of English, (ii) consolidating the correct use of the language the pupils have already acquired, (iii) teaching the conventionally correct forms of the language wherever the pupil has acquired deviated forms due to early circumstances, and (iv) building further knowledge of the language on what the pupil was acquired.

In otherwords the teacher in English medium schools has plenty to do by way of teaching of active structures of the language rather then read and explain a grammar book.

Any one class for grammar should take care of the major structures present in a textbook lesson. What the teacher should aim at here is to help the pupils use the structure in life situations. A reference to Chapter 8 of 'Teaching English in India' would yield the following Steps for a *Grammar Lesson* : (i) *Initial Work*, (ii) *Presentation*, (iii) *Drill*, (iv) *Situational Practice*, (v) *Review Exercises in Writing*, and (vi) *Home-task for writing.*

Such a method takes care of (i) oral proficiency, (ii) conversational language, (iii) active classroom teaching and (iv) writing. Since direct method is recommended here only for thorough skill-oriented learning of the language, the teacher should take care not to over-use *demonstrative techniques* and create boredom in those pupils who have already acquired proficiency over the structures under consideration.

There are numerous aspects of spoken (conversational) English which the teacher should take care of. This cannot always be related to the textbook lessons, but occasional classics should be dedicated to the teaching of spoken English. It is surprising that after learning English in English medium school for over ten years a student is still found possessing very inadequate knowledge of the actual conversational aspects of English. This vacuum should be fulled in by means of classes in spoken English in which the focus should be on *conversational forms*. While teaching a mixed class consisting of pupils from groups (i) and groups (ii), the requirements, of both the groups by adhering to a judicious use of demonstrative techniques (as part of direct method), very limit work on formal grammar in primary classes, and provision for challenging material for work to keep the brighter section of the pupils enthusiastic.

(b) The Teaching of Vocabulary : Vocabulary is an aspect of English which has received least attention as a lesson of its own identity. Teaching vocabulary has got usually lost in the teaching of the textbook lesson or rather as part of the explanatory teaching of the text. No need is usually felt to treat the lexical items separately and to increase the vocabulary stock of the pupils. While reading the text for explanatory work the difficult words are spotted and the pupils are given some kind of crude equivalents explanatory definitions and sentences for illustrations.

Teaching vocabulary as part of teaching English in English medium schools should receive special attention. Lexis forms the bulwark of proficiency in speech and writing. No headway can be made in the mastery over the language unless one's vocabulary store increases considerably. Every pupils is required to have a thorough grounding in general vocabulary by the time he or she is out of school, which will later function as the substratum for building specialized professional vocabulary. An inadequate general vocabulary would render a later professional life useless and make communication difficult. Instead of merely presenting the English or L_1 equivalents of the English words, the teacher of English has a few alternatives at his disposal. Chapter I of T.E.I. gives the teaching steps of vocabulary lesson; it is possible to have several departures if the teacher desires so. If the teacher does not think it necessary to spend one vocabulary lesson each for every lesson in the textbook, it is possible to have a vocabulary lesson for a couple of lessons in the textbook together. But mostly every textbook lesson at any level in an English-medium school will include enough new words to have at least one lesson in vocabulary alone.

The chief purpose of engaging one class in vocabulary alone for every unit is to acquaint the pupils with the new words so much so that they acquire practice in using these words in their own language both orally and in writing. A *vocabulary lesson* in an English medium school can have the following Steps: (i) *Initial Work*, (ii) *Presentation*, (ii) *Drill* (use of the new words in mechanical or set verbal contexts), (iv) *Situational Practice*, (v) *Review Exercises in Writing*, (vi) *Home-task for Writing*. Such a method takes care of (i) introducing the words through demonstrative techniques, (ii) teaching the relevant meaning of the words, (iii) oral work using the new words, and (iv) written work using the new words. The words at one become feasible for the pupil's own use.

(c) The Teaching of Reading : While practically no silent reading is taught in L_1 schools, training is given to pupils in the art of silent and fast reading. Reading for most teachers, as we have seen is reading aloud despite all that is known about silent reading. The teacher reads aloud; and the pupils are also trained in reading aloud. All the theory on silent reading and reading comprehension seldom see the light of the day so far as the teacher of English is concerned, and the usual practice of explanatory reading of the text by the teacher goes on in the classroom.

With all the emphasis put on reading in present circumstances, the teacher of English cannot neglect the *reading skill*, as part of English. The present practice of explanatory reading of the text has to be got rid of. The text is the material form which several *skill-oriented lessons* are drawn as we have examined. Reading is just one skill drawn out of or developed on the basis of the text. Therefore even in English medium schools reading aloud be taught as a separate lesson consisting of its own ordering of techniques. The objective should be, again, to develop the skill to read fast with adequate comprehension of the material.

Like any other language skills it is easy to teach reading because of the high language proficiency level of the pupils in English medium schools. Again, for reason of the language background and higher intelligibility level, the teacher may introduce at some Step (preferably during discussion through questioning) some explanation of the text which seems necessary. This is true especially at the high school level where greater insights into the text is desirable and the teacher can lead the pupils to possible depths of discovery by means of detailed questioning.

A Reading lesson (Intensive Reading) at any level in an English-medium school can have the following Steps: (i) *Initial Work*, including vocabulary if not taught earlier, (ii) *Model Reading* by the teacher, (iii) *Silent Reading* by the pupils, (iv) *Discussion* through questioning and explanation of problem areas for greater insights, (v) *Review exercise in Writing*, (vi) *Home-task* for reading and writing. Silent reading is the main Step in a Reading lesson and would therefore call for special attention from the teacher. Close supervision and guidance during silent reading should help the pupils avoid all sorts of impediments to fast reading and read a given text fast with adequate comprehension of the content matter. Extensive Reading and supplementary (library) reading should have proper place in teaching English in English-medium schools.

(d) ***The Teaching of Composition :*** Composition in English medium schools is often an isolated thing having nothing to do with a given teaching unit, and composition it taught to be identical with writing. Mostly the teacher chooses a topics on the spot, perhaps in consultation with the pupils, and the pupils write a composition on the topic. If a picture is available a discussion may be held preliminary to the composition. Composition by and large is the pupil's work of writing in which the teacher has very limited role to play. Whatever departures made in this regard are limited only to the creative imagination of very resourceful teachers.

Composition in its oral and writing forms is the climax of the work on a given *teaching unit*. Composition even in English medium schools cannot be something isolated form a unit. What begins with structures would end with composition. English medium schools are no exception to this. Again, with all the language proficiency at the disposal of the pupils, the teacher can help work out most effective oral and written composition. Since much importance is already given to writing in other lessons, stress should be put on oral composition in English medium schools at all levels. There should be place for a composition lesson at the end of every unit. This will certainly prove very useful in developing the poser of *expression* in good English. Since classroom involvement is much appreciated by pupils in English medium schools, oral composition provides for considerable verbal involvement by the pupils. Unlike other lessons *oral composition* provides great motivation and satisfaction especially to brilliant pupils while others draw benefits by continually listening to the work done in class. Again, unlike written composition, oral composition helps other take great advantage of sentences constructed by brilliant pupils.

While oral composition is difficult for reasons of inadequate language in the case of pupils in L_1 schools, Oral Composition lessons become a asset in English medium schools can have the following Steps : (i) *Initial Work*, (ii) *Discussion through questioning*, and *developing points*, (iii) *Working out or building* the whole composition by individual pupils on the basis of the points provided for the purpose, and (iv) *Writing the composition* either at home or in another class period. By means of composition significant work can be done to (i) help the slow-learner attain proficiency, and (ii) provide challenging work to the brighter section of the class.

(e) ***The Teaching of Poetry*** : More than at any other place, teachers, of English in English medium schools are concerned with the teaching of poetry, as poetry figures in as a major portion of the English textbooks in English medium schools. Again as usual, poetry is an area which is most carelessly treated; the sole method of teaching poetry in most cases is explanation of the *thematic content* of the poem by the teacher. The method used in such that no distinction in made between the objectives of teaching prose and poetry. The sole purpose at the times turns out to be to draw *morals* out of the poem.

Chapter 12 of T.E.I. discusses how poetry can be effectively taught to suit the needs of particular levels. The English proficiency attained by the pupils of English medium schools enables them to learn and appreciate poetry much more than the pupils of L_2 schools do. With the language background at their disposal these pupils will have greater insight into the language content, thematic content and sound patterns of poetry. Poetry with all its potentials, becomes an *experience* which is precious and rewarding in the context of learning English as a second language. If learning poetry were to become a real experience of deeper value with an awakening of the pupils's *aesthetic sense*, the pupils should have through involvement. Learning poetry should turn out to be more of the pupils' experience than of the teacher. What happens in our schools in fact is that the teacher enjoys reading and explaining a poem instead of helping the pupils understand, enjoy and appreciate the poem themselves. The teacher's creative imagination should work in this direction, rather than lecturing in a language which the pupils neither understand nor care to follow.

A *Poetry lesson* in English medium schools can have the following Steps and variations and possible depending on the individuals teacher's understanding of the objectives: (i) *Initial Work* including teaching of the difficult words which the poem, (ii) *Model recitation* of the poem by the teacher, (iii) *Individual recitation* by a few pupils (ii and iii together would enable the pupils to answer the teacher's questions), (iv) *Discussion* by means of questions on the thematic content, language and sound patterns of the poem, and *explanations* of difficult and important areas of the poem for better insights, (v) *Group recitation* by the pupils. The following are the advantages of the method: (i) pupils have full involvement, (ii) recitation have a major place in the method, (iii) discussion paves way for the pupils to think about the content, language and sound arrangement, and (iv) the teacher is given opportunity to *explain* important areas of the poem. Learning poetry this way is bound to be a pleasure on the part of the pupils.

4. Resourcefulness of English-medium Schools

With all the resources at the disposal of English medium schools, they can work wonders in regard to the teaching of English. There are several such resources which can make English medium schools, mini-centres of English language teaching:

(1) ***Money Resources :*** It may be considered the most significant one as the availability of all the rest highly depends on money. Large sums of money are invested in most well-run English medium schools but to what extent this money is ultimately brought to bear up on the pupil's learning is questionable. Only where proper *personnel* are appointed to take care of and put use the best *equipment* of all sorts purposes of classroom teaching and overall learning experiences will English education adequately prosper.

2. ***Personnel Resources:*** It is possible for English medium schools to attract the best personnel available for several

apparent reasons. But it is indeed a sad fact that very few schools are free from nepotism and business-mindedness. Where well-qualified people are appointed at all levels, the community at once recognised the *qualitative work* done. Whatever be the other resources available, it all fails at the level of poorly equipped and incompetent staff, because the staff functions as the *liaison* between all resources and the pupils. A competent staff can makeup, on the other hand, for much of what is lacking at other levels.

(3) ***Equipment Resources:*** English medium schools do spend large sums of money on equipment at various levels such as building up good libraries. Again, how much for such equipment is properly put to use and to what extent individual teachers are either allowed to or interested in using such specialized equipment are questionable. In most schools we find things such as a tape-recorder or a projector placed as a show-piece and no English teacher or others can have access to such a thing for fear of such things being damaged or misused. All such things are kept as pieces of exhibition for visitors. Until this situation changes teaching English in English medium schools will tend to continue to be mere verbal gymnastics with the teacher unable to put his heart and sound into effective teaching. With all such varied recourses English mediums schools to enhance English education in our country despite all political prejudices.

13
Equipping the English Teacher

1. Adequate Teacher Education Programmes

There is no use finding fault with pupils, teachers or systems for the kind of inadequacy that present-day education as a whole and English teaching in particular levels. The tremendous gap between policy-making on the one hand and adequate implementation of programmes on the other seem to be the principal cause for most of the failures. If the generations of learners are to be *well-equipped* with English language, then the teaching population require adequate training follow-up programmes and necessary *resources* to equip the learners. This in turn reflects ultimately on the *planning* and *implementation* of adequate programmes at the teacher education centres.

What the present-day centres of teacher education are doing tis to react to and cope with a changing situation rather than positively reconstruct *institutional planning* and bring about fundamental reforms. Highly utopian programmes are planned and recommended for institutional reforms but nothing stands implemented on the basis of purely academic interests. Whatever innovations are usually brought about do not have any far reaching resonance on the practical work carried out in an institution but limit themselves to vested institutional interests. A close look into an institution for teacher education where the *teacher of English* is trained and equipped, the following aspects which require constant innovation can be demarcated fairly clearly;

1. The selection policies for admission of candidates to the institution, which require revision in regard to the changing circumstances.
2. The planning of the curricular activities which require change as year go by.
3. The organisation and administration of the curricular activities to see that things go as per the planning and recommendations.
4. The planning, organization and administration of whatever co-curricular activities expected to be undertaken during the year.
5. The *extension service* considered parallel to the work of the institution, in which the student-teachers may have some vital role to play.
6. The programmes that take care of the daily, weekly, monthly, and termwise work of the institutions.
7. The policies that govern the institution's system of student *evaluation*, teacher evaluation, institutional evaluation, and systems evaluation as part of the overall programme.
8. The system of *teaching practices* and other practical orientations provided to the candidates.
9. The system of *practice teaching* undertaken by the student-teacher as part of the requirements for his degree in Education.
10. The stress put on the *content* part of the course in English language teaching methods.
11. The correlation established between the teaching methodology for English and other courses offered as part of the general course in Education.
12. A core course in *general methodology* which would enable the teacher to be effective in subjects other than what he is specialized in.

13. The mode of *personal guidance* the teacher-supervisors are required to give as part of the training in the institutions; and
14. The mode of *lesson planning*, preparation, teaching, supervision, and assessment expected to take place as part of the course.

A part from the aspects of the training programme mentioned above, there are several other important elements that require constant checking, assessment of efficiency and revision when required. Among these are : preparation of teaching aids, instructional material, auto-instructional material, test material for English, internal submission of various kinds related directly to the teaching of English, preparation of action research projects etc. A timely revision, if not radical innovation, of everyone of these aspects is required of the institution for teacher education if worthwhile preparation of the student-teacher has to be properly brought about.

The teacher of English at the time of his training in *English language teaching methodology* should receive attention in the following aspects of the teacher's role in the teaching of English in school:

1. However ill-equipped an educational institution may be, the greatest priority should go to the development of language proficiency in the student-teachers, something which, sad to say, the schools and colleges have not succeeded in taking care of.
2. The student-teacher require some background in phonetics, linguistics and psycho-linguistics as part of the general background for the study of language as such; he needs a course in the structure of English with stress on English syntax, and requires the study of education, psychology, and aspects of school administration as part of his general course in education.
3. The most important aspect of his training in the institution is his acquaintance with English language teaching methodology which will render him great service in his professional life.

4. As part of the general training he requires the knowledge of preparation of instructional and test materials and teaching aids; he should be in a position to set a good question paper and evaluate his pupils performance.
5. The theory should emerge from practice; the teaching of English right from lesson planning upto the teacher's follow-up work after classroom teaching should find place in the practical work.
6. The teacher is an investigator; the trend should be established in the institution itself through ample training in action research with very practical implications.
7. Above all, work in the institution should be oriented to helping the teacher obtain a harmonious co-ordination of *language, content, methods* and *values*. This co-ordination determines the teacher's success in his later professional life.

2. In-service Programmes for Teachers

It is all right that much is done, perhaps, for the preparation of teachers of English in institutions of education. All the same, the teachers who go out of such institutions and serve in schools for years together stand greatly in need of what we call *in-service courses* of serval types. By in-service courses, we therefore mean, the training the teacher receives while he is in service. If the pre-service training in education and English teaching is to remain effective on the individual teacher, then such intensive in-service courses are urgent necessity. Of the day to improve the English language teaching scene. The intension is not to make ELT experts out of teachers, but the following may be considered the principal objectives of in-service courses for teacher of English.

1. In-service courses aim at familiarizing the teacher with the *latest trends* and developments in the area of ELT and make his knowledge of ELT so up to date as to become beneficial to him in his classroom teaching.
2. In-service courses in the form of *refresher courses* help him update what he learned from the institution of education which will be at his disposal to enhance his classroom practices.

3. In-service courses aim at boosting the English teacher's self-confidence in the teaching of English, by sharing his views, successes and failures with those of his profession, who project parallel experiences.
4. The regular course in education followed by regular teaching in school followed by in-service courses of some kind has great advantages to enable the teacher relate *theory and practice* against the background of the practical problems he confronts in actual teaching situations in school.
5. In-service courses are all not mere refresher courses, and as such they increases the teacher's *formal qualifications* to stand eligible for better treatment in his school as a teacher of English.
6. In-service courses make up for what is lacking in the usual programmes in regular institutions of education, by offering intensive courses in phonetics, linguistics, psycholinguistics socio-linguistics and English teaching methodology, Such subjects are not usually offered as part of the training the teacher receives in institutions of education.
7. In-services courses, again, help educationists and those involved in extension services assess a given situation in regard to the performance of teachers of English, their aptitudes and creative abilities of teachers of English.

The advantages of in-service courses are several for the teacher of English to excel in his profession. In-service courses enable to be aware of his dignity and roles as a teacher, find on-the-spot solutions to the practical classroom problems he faces, adjust himself better to the school environment which, perhaps, pose considerable problems for him, and lastly recognize the role of other as teachers and know with sympathy the problems of his colleagues as teachers of English. Thus the greatest service which in-service courses can render the teacher is to make his fully aware of his *professional life* which otherwise tends to become a routine with unpredictable consequences.

In-service courses may be of several useful types :

(i) *Refresher courses* which are meant to be a revision of what he is expected to have done during his formal training;

(ii) *Summer institutes* which are meant further enlighten the teacher with the latest trends in ELT scene;

(iii) *Orientation courses* which help his with the practical aspects of, say, teaching grammar or writing, which are not meant to acquaint him with the latest theoretical stands;

(iv) *Seminars* in which experts in ELT present papers for the teachers of English and enlighten them on selected aspects of ELT ; and

(v) *Workshops* in which the teachers of English can be active role to play and have an occasion to share the views and experiences with others of his profession. All said and done, in-service curses depend for their success entirely on the motives which ultimately guide the sponsors of such programmes, and the teachers who participate in such programmes.

3. The Teacher and Social Feed-back

An important factor which cannot be overlooked in connection with the *efficient functioning* of the English teacher is the type and degree of social feed-back he receives in return. It is not only the institutions of education and the school that equip the teacher but also the community of which the school forms a part has a moral obligation to equip the teacher by means of proper social feed-back. It is significant that we discuss this aspect in this connection. Just as the teacher of English is a person dedicated to the cause of the community, the community in its turn should have things in store for the teacher in whose hands is endowed the future of the learners.

The social feed-back that the teacher receives is different in kind, and degree from community to community. The following types may be found among communities in regard to the way they treat teacher:

(1) There are communities where the teacher is a well-respected and dignified person no matter what socio-economic level he belongs to. The teacher, for economic reasons, is not a

highly paid public servant; but the absence of satisfactory pay is compensated for by the respective community in terms of the dignified treatment the teacher is given.

(2) There are those communities where the teacher is considered just another public servant who does the work of teaching as anybody else say, as a clerk. The teacher here may or may not be paid well but no special dignity is attached to the profession which others do not command. He is not motivated unlike anyone else because of the special call of a teacher he has received.

(3) Lastly, there are those communication which consider the teaching profession much less dignified because as a teacher one comparably earns very little. These are communities which attach a great deal to of importance to monatarily productive professions and occupations. The teacher is just a common man, no better than an educated servant who takes care of one's children.

The three situations we have examined above are very relevant to our country and, perhaps, the three are rather exhaustive types in relation to the dignity they attach to the profession of teaching. Whatever the present situations may be, one thing is true that the teacher's profession cannot have greater impact on the community unless great value is attached with it. The teacher of English, as one endowed with a responsibility to mould future generations in terms of language proficiency cannot function satisfactorily and efficiently unless he is properly *recognized*, his work *valued*, and his qualifications and abilities *respected* in the community. The greatest *feed-back* is for him, the recognition, social acceptance as a teacher and a special dignity that should invariably go with the teacher's profession. If the profession of teaching were to attract the cream of society, one thing is certain that a lot more of these should form part of it.

The whole point has another dimension also. The teacher of English in present-day circumstances if highly required to *project a clear image* for him to be recognized by society. In a social set up where all categories of people from all walks of life competently contribute to the manifold progress of society, the teacher has no right to be complacent about what he has acquired and what he does. If only the teacher stands upto the challenges he confronts, can he hope for any recognition in his community. More than any other section of the teaching community, the teacher of English today stands lonely because his in a controversial profession in the developing present-day political climate. It is going to be worse if the so-called teacher of English is incapable of uttering one correct sentence in English. Can a community be expected to respect and welcome one who does not possess even the most elementary aptitudes that render him useful to the community the way it expects. The image that the teacher receives back is perhaps the same image he himself projects like the reflection in a mirror.

4. The Teacher and Self-Education

There is certainly no doubt that all said and done the teacher of English is ultimately responsible for the predicament in which he finds himself because in any given situation there is ample scope for self-education on the part of the teacher. No one can deny that self-education is rewarding one way or other and that it is a continuing thing rather than a matter of a given period of time. What is self-education ? It is the manner in which a teacher equips himself in the following cases:

1. The teacher of English endeavours to keep himself abreast with the latest trends in English language teaching by reading the available lot of books and periodicals dealing with the subject.
2. The teacher meets those whom he considers resource personnel in the teaching of English and gets enlightened about aspects of ELT which have posed problems for him.
3. The teacher is eager to share his views and experiences in ELT with his friends so that there is a constant give and take which keep his professional spirit high.
4. As a teacher of English he is required to know several things related to the teaching of English; he develops an eagerness to read veraciously on such subjects so that both his classroom teaching and his contacts with those of his profession will remain fruitful.
5. Lastly, self-education means an awareness to receive and

assimilate whatever is positively new in a spirit of continuous research so that the teacher when confronted as usual with problems in or outside his class will not turn back disappointed, but will be equipped to meet such situations squarely and find proper solutions. Self-education is oriented to the analysis of problem situations of all sorts with an inquisitive bend of mind, and much help is drawn in this regard by the teacher from the *resources* of (i) his own professional experience, and (ii) his continuous acquaintence with people, books and periodicals.

Self-education, again has three distinct dimensions : *content*, *method*, and *values*.

1. *Content :* An area where self-education is very much required is the content part of English language teaching. It should be called the most important because no one can ever hope to master the whole of English language, its linguistics, phonetics, its literature and several other theoretical considerations. The teacher on his own endeavours to be continually in search of new material with a view to enhancing his teaching experiences and to equip himself professionally. No one can satisfactorily respond to the growing mass of literature in aspects related to English language teaching and education as a whole, but sincere attempts on the part of the teacher will certainly have far reaching resonances in his teaching work. Continual mastery of English language is the foundation upon which everything else rests.

2. *Method* : The second area where the teacher of English is required to have self-education in the method and techniques of teaching English. The training in teaching methods which the teacher received from the institutions of education is only the foundation and the general framework of what he is expected to do in the classroom. On his turn, the teacher concretely experiments with his knowledge of the method in his classroom, renders his information concrete, modifies what he learned and synthesizes in an eclectic manner what several experts have said about teaching. The result is

that the teacher *evolves a method* adequate to meet the requirements of the concrete situation in which he lives. This is the most effective self-education he is expected to have in regard to his teaching methodology as a teacher of English.

3. *Values*: The third area where the teacher requires self-education is the set of values which as teacher he is expected to cherish. Content and methods are important; but the teacher should be guided in all this by a set of adequate values which only will give him adequate motivation and satisfaction in work. The teacher is a professional and has interpersonal communion with the rest of his community. The community expects him to behave, believe things in a manner that suits his profession. *A dedicated, committed* and *sincere* teacher who does not go by the norm of *profit* or *flattery* is loved by the community. The teacher of English needs to project a *value-guided image*.

5. Aspects of Practice-teaching

Lastly, we need to consider practice-teaching as an aspect of teacher education meant principally to train the student-teacher in methods of teaching English and to acquaint him in advance with what he would later confront in the school situation as a regular teacher of English. Practice-teaching is the most important period and aspect of teacher education which functions like a *rehearsal* when the student-teacher receives his professional instructions in relation to his performance as a classroom practitioner. Practice-teaching does not consist in a set of theoretical instruction, but it is a matter of *skill, practice* and *training*. Some people call it a 'battle innoculation' to strengthen the teacher to face the classroom as a regular teacher and fightout his professional battle. Teaching should no longer frighten him or make him nervous.

Practice-teaching puts the student-teacher right in the midst of pupils and the school. It creates for him the same situations as he is going to face in the school later. Practice-teaching given at various levels doesn't intend to make a perfect teacher; instead it puts him right in the portals of a school situation and makes a beginning for him to function as a teacher. Therefore it may be called a process of *initiation* into teaching. It can very well be called a short *internship* just as the medical practitioner is expected to undergo. As part of the teacher's pre-service education programme, practice-teaching is almost the climax of his activities in the institution of education when he performs the role of a teacher in the classroom.

The aims of practice-teaching can be listed in the following manner:

1. The student teacher should be provided with congenial conditions to control his behaviour. Only under such conditions can his behaviour specificities be *observed, analyzed* and *studied*. As a result changes can be recommended in concrete behavioural situations.
2. Teaching is a role-play; the teacher requires plenty of opportunity to manipulate his potentialities in playing his role. Teaching-practice enables him right in the realm of the classroom to play and practice his role as a teacher.
3. Practice-teaching takes place in schools; as such he views the school as a student. There are new problems, new challenges and new satisfactions which he as a student never experienced.
4. Practice-teaching opens for the student-teacher new vistas of knowledge and experience which at the institution of education he would never have. He is student there; it is a transformation into the experiences of a teacher.
5. Practice-teaching provides him with ample opportunity to test his own adequacy as a teacher which would be the biggest help in making a decision as to whether or not accept the call as a teacher. Merely joining the institution of education does not guarantee that he is capable of functioning as a teacher or if he will derive proper professional satisfaction. Although certainly changes are possible, the candidate receives the first glimpse of actual work in the classroom and school during practice-teaching.
6. Practice-teaching more than at many other time enables the institution of education to assess the student's performance

as a teacher. In fact practice-teaching should receive the maximum possible stress since it tells the institution not how clever the teacher is going to be but how fit he is to function as an effective teacher.

7. Practice-teaching is the time when the student-teacher acquaints himself with the manifold co-curricular programmes of the school, which he as a regular teacher will be called on to look after.

Practice-teaching is not carried out in all institutions in one and the same manner. There are several *ways of organizing* practice-teaching:

1. In certain cases there are *bloch-teaching* and *off-campus* programmes. Practice lessons in this context takes place in two phases. A certain number of lessons are given by the candidate does not stay throughout. Here concentration is on the *lessons* rather than on the student-teacher's overall involvement in the programmes of the school. It is the first attempt of the student-teacher in giving lessons in a regular class, and consequently closer supervision is expected than would takeplace during the off-campus programme. The '*off-campus* takesplace in a school where the student-teachers are expected to stay on and involve themselves in all the activities of the school. It is a fairly intense programme and the candidates are kept busy in matters related to teaching.
2. In other cases, there is no off-campus programmes, instead the lessons are given in a local school where the student-teachers involve themselves in all possible activities. The lessons in such instances may be given in blochs or fairly distributed. Much depend on the facility available and the attitude of the school-authorities in making themselves adjusted to the teaching programme.
3. The third way of doing it is to give all the required lessons not in any local schools but in a fairly distant place where the candidates make it an off-campus programme. There are several ways in which the duration of each programme may be arranged depending on the particular situation in which the institution of education finds itself. All the same there are a definite number of lessons which the candidates are

required to complete before they obtain the degree in education.

There are certain set of norms which can make practice-teaching highly effective in achieving its goals:

1. Practice-teaching should be a continuous process where the student-teacher feels that he is involved in regular teaching rather than a co-curricular activity which form just another part of the education programme.
2. The teacher goes by units while taking teaching in a class; he is aware that a lesson in the textbook is not any isolated thing but a complex of several types of classroom-lessons.
3. The supervision should take care of the detailed aspects of every lesson rather than judging it from an overall performance.
4. The candidate should feel that the practice-lessons he gives are the concrete models based on which he will be able to teach later in his school.
5. He should involve himself in other activities of the school where he gives the lessons. It is rare chance at his disposal the advantages of which he will realize only when he becomes a regular teacher.
6. A day's lessons should precede proper instructions from the supervisor and should be followed by a session meant to evaluate and review the day's work.
7. Select guidance should be given in regard to classroom interaction, a point which should not be neglected.

Practice-teaching has been oriented to *micro-teaching* proper; on rather micro-teaching has gradually been made part of the practice-teaching programme. Instead of the present macro-classroom lessons, the student-teachers may have micro-lessons in the school with the result that concentration on several component teaching abilities of the candidate is made possible. How far such a thing is possible outside the walls of the institution of education is open to question. The desirability of micro-teaching as part of regular classroom teaching is questioned by many. At the same time one thing is certain, there are possibilities of micro-lessons being made integral part of practice-teaching:

1. Micro-teaching should be undertaken during practice-teaching as a *preparation* for the student-teacher's scheduled classroom teaching.
2. Micro-teaching may not always require *pupils* from the classroom as noted in the chapter on 'Micro-teaching' (Ch.13.). Micro-teaching can be undertaken with the student-teachers themselves playing the role of pupils. But whenever possible it is advisable to get a group of pupils for micro-lessons, to render the situation natural and effective.
3. Micro-lessons may not *substitute* actual classroom lessons because the aims of both are very different. Micro-lessons can only be at most an adequate preparation for regular classroom lessons. Micro-lessons aim at perfecting the teacher's teaching habits, but classroom lessons aim at developing the learner's language habits.
4. Where facilities are available a particular class of pupils may be divided into small groups and several student-teachers at a time can take up one micro-unit or other and have ample practice with other student-teachers helping him in the absence of the supervisor.

Micro-teaching, by and large should form the chief preparation for actual classroom lessons and supplement rather than substitute regular classroom lessons as the requirement for the degree in education. Practice-teaching is intended to be a *welcome experience* rather than a nightmare, and the student-teachers have to be positively oriented to approach classroom teaching with pleasure. It is so unique as to leave sometimes permanent marks on the individual person's future relations with pupils, and the classroom.

14
Micro-teaching in Teacher Education

1. Micro-teaching as a Method of Teacher-education

Teacher-educators have been on the look out in recent times for evolving a method of training student-teachers, which would invariably raise the lot above the morass of present-day teacher training methods. All said and done we stand still on the same old ways of practice-teaching, training in methods and supervision. *Micro-teaching* as a method of teacher-education with special reference to classroom teaching has been capable of revolutionising the present approach to teacher-education methods. There has been an ever growing awareness in regard to the vague and undefined way student teachers are introduced to (i) the aspects of *classroom interaction*, (ii) *steps* of teaching specific lessons, (iii) *techniques* employed in classroom teaching, (iv) *evaluation* devices, and (v) methods of proper feed-back in classroom teaching.

Despite knowledge of the lesson as a complex of several sub-components consisting of steps of the lesson, teaching techniques, and the teacher's attitudes, the *traditional methods* of introducing the student-teachers into these systems and training them in the systems have remained ambiguous and unspecified. For instance in the present system of teacher-education there is no provision made to introduce and train the teacher in the art of questioning as a classroom technique. Even after giving numerous lessons in English as required the student-teacher of English remains ineffective in questioning as a teaching technique. In the same way seldom is any specific work done to train the student-teacher in the non-verbal or verbal techniques of *feed-back* in the classroom.

In present-day methods of teacher-education what is done is an attempt to introduce to and train the student-teacher in working on a lesson, *i.e.* teaching a lesson as a whole without even rousing on his part of consciousness of the integral structural components that can render the total lesson a failure if the student-teacher does not develop his faculties in this regard. The unresourceful and incompetent candidate is blamed and harassed because his total lesson, for that matter, is a failure. It is only the *total lesson* that the supervisor and student-teacher is aware of rather than the inherent components i.e., the manifold *techniques* and devices that render the totality of the lesson a success or a failure. The supervisor himself finds no way of redeeming the case because the unity of the trained in stand on the way of his realisation of the truth.

Micro-teaching as a method of teacher-education takes care of the component *abilities*, *techniques* and *steps* of teaching as *micro-units* with a view to equipping the student-teacher with all possible *component abilities* required for classroom practices. The idea is to work on components elements as micro-units and concentrate on such units of a lesson so that both the supervisor as well as the student-teacher will not lose sight of the component units in the context of the totality of a lesson.

Along with the concentrated effort to enhance the component teaching abilities of the student-teacher, another major contribution of micro-teaching lies in the area of the personal attention on the teacher himself. In micro teaching what is *micro* are (i) the *skill*, ability, or aspect of the lesson on which exclusive attention rests, (ii) the *duration* in which the student-teacher works on the specific aspect of the lesson, (iii) the sub-components of the skill which are taken care of *e.g.*, gesticulation while questioning, and more than anything else there is another micro-aspect which is the student-teacher himself. For reasons of the characteristic nature of micro teaching the individual student-teacher receives personal attention much more than he would receive in present-day programmes when several significant *be-havioural components* of the person go quite unnoticed. In the regular supervision the teacher-supervisor loses sight of several important aspects of the person's classroom behaviour but when it comes to micro-teaching these aspects take predominance and receive attention, with the consequence that the student-teacher receives the satisfaction and feed-back greater that what he would otherwise receive.

Micro-teaching, thus does not mean teaching a small class or teaching a short teaching unit. Micro-teaching is a method of *training teachers* in the component skills, abilities, techniques, and steps of an English lesson. It is not a method of teaching English to students of any level. It is possible to have micro-lessons without the regular students at all. The focus is not on the pupils or on their performance, but the teacher who performs with a view to demonstrating and getting trained in certain well defined teaching techniques such as say, *questioning*, or steps of the lesson, say, *presentation*. For this purpose it is good to have a small group of other student-teachers substituting the regular class, with the advantage that (i) it ensures greater participation by them in responding to the student-teacher's questions, and (ii) it increases his confidence in facing a class once he confronts and teaches a class consisting of his own friends who are said to be more critical than one's subordinates or superiors. *An Evaluation Scale* has been included at the end of every type of micro-lesson. It is almost a process of re-orienting the student-teacher's atti-tudes to teaching itself.

2. Micro-lessons on Classroom Techniques : the Classical Approach:

It was recognised that Micro-teaching as a teacher-education method could very well be based on the *classroom techniques* such as questioning or narration. This approach to micro-teaching based on classroom techniques has come to be called 'the classical micro-teaching' which remained prevalent upto the early 80's. Then came the day of 'mini-lessons' or 'mini-micro-teaching based on the steps of teaching or stages that constitute a grammar lesson or a vocabulary lesson (See. Sec. 3.). The present section intends to show the details of what has been called 'micro-teaching.'

Classroom teaching is a *skill* and an *art*; as skill it requires change in a number of *component habits* and inoculation of adequate habits required to make certain techniques successful. But as art, classroom teaching depends very much on the *creative* resources of the teacher in whose hands the classroom techniques assume a new perfection. Micro-teaching is a factor potent enough to add to both the skill and art dimensions of classroom techniques. The following teaching techniques can form material for micro-lessons on techniques. Eventhough for purposes of clarity and adequacy every techniques is treated separately, it is advisable in actual teaching to combine more than one technique for demonstration in micro-teaching. The techniques, for that matter are far too many to receive attention as individual micro-units forming material for micro-lessons.

(1) ***Questioning:*** Questioning can form adequate material for micro-lessons because of the prominence 'questioning' takes as a language teaching technique. Upon analysis one finds that questioning as a technique has several *component features* such as (a) its *framing*, (b) *content matter*, (c) the manner of *distribution* in class, (d) the teacher's *attitudes* in getting responses, (e) the *feed-back* given upon receiving the responses, (f) the teacher's use of *gestures*, (g) the way questions are *revised* when not understood by pupils, (h) the teacher's move when a number of pupils together *do not respond* to the question etc. There are numerous aspects that the student-teacher and the supervisor can pay attention to in a micro-lesson on questioning. An *Evaluation Scale* for lesson on Questioning may include the following aspects: (1) *framework*, (ii) *distribution*, (iii) *relevance*, (iv) *specificity*, and (v) *Clarity*.

(2) ***Verbal Illustration:*** A micro-lesson on verbal illustration as a classroom teaching technique will train a candidate in a number of aspects which form component features of verbal illustration: (a) *adequacy* of the verbal situation used, (b) *duration* taken by the teacher to bring relevant concept, (c)

the correctness of language, (d) *gestures* and *facial expressions* used, (c) *rapport* with the pupils, (f) attention commanded etc.. An *Evaluation Scale* for a micro-lesson in verbal illustration would include: (i) *Adequacy*, (ii) *clarity*, (iii) *relevance*, (iv) *language* (v) *attention*, and (vi) *gestures*.

(3) ***Demonstration :*** A micro-lesson on demonstration as a classroom technique which the teacher is required to use very often, can train the student-teacher in the following component features of demonstrations: (a) *the relevance* of the demonstrative technique for the concept to be conveyed to the pupils, (b) the *simplicity* of the object, or action employed for demonstration, (c) the *clarity* of demonstration for the pupils, (d) the *attention* and interest commanded by the teacher, (e) the *correctness* of the language used, (f) the acceptable and *natural* way the demonstration is made etc. An *Evaluation Scale* for the micro-lesson on demonstration as a technique would include: (i) *relevance*, (ii) *clarity*, (iii) *attention*, (iv) language and (v) *duration*.

Apart from the techniques mentioned above, the chapter on 'Techniques for Teaching English' (Ch. 10) includes a great variety of techniques which at some time or other figure in the various types of English lessons. Micro-lessons may be organised to demonstrate techniques such as the following:

(4) ***Dramatization*** for which can be used an Evaluation Scale which includes features such as : (a) simplicity, (b) adequacy, (c) pupil involvement, (d) language, (e) duration, (f) attention, and (g) feed-back;

(5) ***Miming*** for which the Evaluation Scale would include features such as : (a) originality, (b) simplicity, (c) relatedness, (d) duration, and (e) attention;

(6) ***Narration*** for which the Evaluation Scale could include component features such as (a) fluency, (b) correctness, (c) continuity, (d) structure, (e) clarity, (f) gestures, (g) voice, (h) rapport and (i) duration.

Just as the teacher's activities in the classroom during teaching are definable in terms of certain set of *classroom techniques* on which the teacher depends for the success of his work, the teaching techniques on the other hand are further definable on the basis of the *component features* which go into the making of every technique. It is on the basis of these component features (abilities or skills as used above) that we observe the teacher's abilities, *train* him and *evaluate* his performance. Micro-lessons are meant exclusively to help the student-teacher attain mastery over the effective use of component features that make up every step of teaching and every technique for classroom practices. The supervisor taking care of micro-lessons is required to pay attention to these micro-aspects of the candidate's lesson and help them perform effectively in the micro-classroom primarily, and subsequently in the regular classroom.

3. Mini-lessons Based on Steps of Teaching

The classical micro-teaching is based on classroom techniques. All the same it was felt that the approach had a number of deficiencies. Micro-lessons were allocated only 5 or 6 minutes. The micro-cycles happened to be very cumbersome and largely ineffective in actual practice. Again, evaluation of the lesson because of its complex nature became difficult. Thus it was gradually felt that 'classroom techniques' should be substituted with 'step of teaching' *i.e.* a step such as 'presentation' should form the content of a micro-lesson rather than a technique such as 'questioning.' The new practice allotted to the lessons a duration of 10 minutes and came to be called 'mini-lessons, or mini-micro-teaching.'

'*Teaching English in India*' in detail deals with the structure of various kinds of English lessons attempting to take care of specific aspects of language such as grammar. In all those lessons, as illustrated, it should be seen that the attention is on the lesson as a *total unit* (the advantages of this approach we shall examine in Section 4). All the same, everyone of the lessons consists of a number of specified and well-defined teaching-steps without which the lessons tend to become too general, undefined and confusing. The steps which define the lesson in some way have a lot to do with the very nature of the skill on which the lesson is based (*e.g.*, speaking) and the aspect of language which forms the content matter of the lesson (*e.g.*, vocabulary).

Instead of wanting the student-teacher to present an entire lesson based on a skill and further using a textbook lesson as the material, *micro-teaching* attempts to take care of such lessons in terms of the *specific teaching steps*. For present purposes we shall note the steps of teaching in general as applicable to all the lessons discussed earlier without treating the lessons separately on the basis of the aspects of language which form the material of every lesson. Micro-teaching takes care of the following *teaching steps* with a view of helping the student-teacher develop his component skills and techniques as related to each teaching step:

(1) **Step — 1:**

Initial Work : The first step of teaching an English lesson is the Initial Work, also known as preliminary work, preparation, motivation etc. (Ch. 10). Drawing the student-teacher away from the notion of a 'total lesson' for a while, micro-teaching attempts to focus all attention on the various component aspects of Initial Work *i.e.*, the *Initial Works* of (i) Spoken English Lesson, (ii) Structure Lesson, (iii) Vocabulary Lesson, (iv) Intensive Reading Lesson, (v) Extensive Reading Lesson, (vi) Oral Composition Lesson, (vii) Written composition Lesson, and (viii) Poetry Lesson. Throughout the present section reference will be made only to the (Eight) types of lessons mentioned above without specifying every lesson. The respective chapters dealing with the lessons include the various aspects of Initial Work. A micro-lesson on Initial Work will train a student teacher on the following aspects: (i) the *techniques* employed during the work (*e.g.* questioning, dramatization etc.), (ii) the rapport the teacher has established during the work, (iii) the *feedback* the teacher has provided, (iv) the *language* used, (v) the *gestures* which formed part of his teaching, (vi) the teacher' attempts to get proper *responses* from the pupils and whole lot of other aspects all of which together make up what we call the Initial Work. *An Evaluation Scale* for Initial Work should include at least: (i) *relevance*, (i) *continuity*, (iii) *technique*, (iv) *language*. These four could form, apart from those mentioned above, specific points for the evaluation of a micro-lesson on Initial Work.

(2) **Step — 2**:

Presentation/Development/Recitation: As we have examined in the relevant chapters on types of English lessons, the Spoken English, Structure and Vocabulary lessons have *presentation* as the second step, and the composition lessons have *development*; while the poetry lesson has *recitation* as the second step. The step 2 of an English lesson on the basis of some specification such as 'presentation of structure' is focussed in a micro-lesson and helps the student-teacher on the one hand *reveal* his skill in handling the step and on the other *learn* proper ways of teaching in Step 2. A micro-lesson, thus should take care of aspects such as : (i) the *techniques* employed, (ii) *interaction* devices used, (iii) the *adequacy* of language, (iv) the *correctness* of language, (v) the progress of teaching and (vi) the non-verbal devices used by the teacher. An *evaluation scale* for Step 2 should include: (i) *techniques*, (ii) *clarity*, (iii) *progress*, (iv) *attention*, (v) language, and (vi) *aids* and *chalkboard work*.

(3) **Step — 3 (+4)** :

Practice/Discussion/Discourse-Construction : An examination of the relevant chapters on the types of lessons would show that Step.3 differs from lesson to lesson. Some involve 'practice', other 'discussion' or 'discourse-construction.' A micro-lesson on the Step. 3 part of an English lesson has several aspects of take care of. The step is a complex of aspects and skills such as (i) the *techniques* used, (ii) the adequacy of *language*, (iii) pupil *involvement*, (iv) the *rapport* established, (v) the intensity of drill, and (vi) the adequacy of the *situations* introduced. *An Evaluation Scale* would include: (i) *techniques*, (ii) *pupil participation*, (iii) *drill*, (vi) *application*, (v) *situational adequacy* and (vi) *Teaching aids*.

(4) **Step — 4: (+5):**

Review/Recitation: The step 4 for an English lesson differs, again depending on the type of lesson it is. While a structure lesson has 'Review' in Step. 5, a poetry lesson includes 'Recitation' as the fourth step. A micro-lesson on the Step 4 of any lesson should include: (i) the *techniques* used, (ii) the student *response*, (iii) the *rapport* established, (iv) the *feed-back* provided, (v) the language used in the review. An *evaluation scale* for Review would include : (i) *techniques*, (ii) *language*, (iii) *validity*, (iv) *link*, and (v) pupils' *response*.

The micro-lesson on teaching steps attempts to achieve three things: (i) *observe* the individual student-teacher's component teaching abilities, (ii) *train* the person in essential component abilities, and (iii) *evaluate* the person's performance in terms of his component abilities. Observation of what habits the student-teacher possesses, adequate training in the formation of required habits and evaluation of his subsequent performance can be considered the principal target of micro-teaching. While teaching each 'Step of teaching' has to be concretely related to a basic skill and an aspect of language such as the *presentation* part of a *vocabulary* lesson in which the *listening-speaking* skill predominates.

4. The Supervisor's Role in Mini-microteaching

There is a world of difference that exists between mini-lessons and regular teaching. This difference can easily defeat all the lofty purposes of mini-microteaching. Regular lessons are taught in a regular classroom and number of factors make a lesson serious, well-intended and purposeful. First, the lessons are taught in a regular school, regular classroom and the immediate aim is actually to teach a group of pupils rather than for the student teacher to obtain practice. The student teacher is functioning as a regular teacher and he is *not simulating* any teaching situation. There is an added dimension of responsibility that go with the regular classroom which the student teacher or his supervisor at the back of the class cannot shirk. These aspects make regular classroom teaching a very serious and responsible affair.

But a mini-lesson has a world of difference. It's all taught in *unreal, simulated situations* that have been formally created only for the student teacher's practice. The class consists of the peer-group; the content of teaching doesn't aim at *any teaching at all*; there is no actual teaching taking place: whatever is happening in the mini-class is simulated only for the student teacher's training. This world of unreality can all crash and fall to pieces if the student teacher as well as the supervisor who is coordinating the teaching lose sight of their objective and take the whole matter lightly. In such cases mini-microteaching can easily turnout to be a big force.

This major danger can be avoided only by means of enlightened and well-intended supervision. Hence the supervisor's role in mini-microteaching cannot be overstressed It all depends how seriously he coordinated the entire thing and guides the teacher student in the course of the lesson. This calls for special training for the teacher educator in order to supervise mini-lessons. The supervisor has several roles to play and several things to do.

1. Mini-microteaching begins with planning. The supervisor sees to it that a correct and challenging unit is selected by the *sub-group* that may consist of three or four students for planning the three or four *different steps* of a lesson such as *composition* or *grammar*. The supervision should ensure that the student-teacher knows that he is just a simulating a regular lesson, and that he is working on such a small and seemingly unimportant matter such as 'the Preparation Step' of a lesson because he is only simulating actual teaching situation. He should ensure that the planning is based on a correct understanding of the structure of a regular lesson of which the mini-lesson is only a part.
2. The supervisor has got to be most alert in the course of the lesson. The *simulated work* goes on only for ten minutes. The supervisor is present there not as an examiner to silently evaluate the student's performance. Instead he is *more of a guide* and this role is very significant. As a guide he keenly and in a present-minded manner watches the entire structure and presentation of the lesson with interest. He looks for the following aspects:
   (i) the student's language, both the language of instructions and the aspect being taught,
   (ii) the aptness of the techniques involved,
   (iii) the pupil's response to each technique,
   (iv) the organisation of the techniques under the particular

step of the lesson,

(v) the teacher's attitude towards the class,

(vi) the range of feedback he is using,

(vii) the pupil involvement he is initiating,

(viii) the clarity of presentation, and lastly

(ix) the teacher's awareness.

of the mini-lesson as being only a single step, knit into a whole, regular lesson. This 'holistic awareness' is central to the fact that the student teacher is only simulating.

3. Apart from providing apt and lucid comments in the student's journal the supervisor provides *on the spot guidance* in case of serious deviations, departures or errors. He makes sure that the deviation affects the whole texture of the lesson and that the lesson is not disturbed while correcting him. Wherever possible the supervisor organises a *feedback session* immediately after one round of the various steps of a lesson is completed by a team. This can be very short and cute and can take care of several aspects of their teaching. The supervision part of the mini-microteaching is a big role to play chiefly because the whole thing is unreal, simulated, artificial and sensitive; all the same micro-teaching is perhaps the best solution to the problem of cumbersome practice teaching programmes.

5. Effective Organisation of Mini-microteaching

As teaching in simulated conditions, mini-lessons need to be organised with meticulous care in order to avoid careless handling of the work. Mini-micro-teaching as a teacher education method organised under simulated conditions has a number of week points:

Classroom teaching or regular classroom lessons have a unity or integrity which if destroyed loses much of what we hope to get out of them. Mini-lessons are incapable of providing this total perspective of a classroom lesson. Any number of mini-lessons will not give the student teacher this total perspective of a regular classroom lesson with its dimension of realism and seriousness. One would never imagine teaching a regular class the

'Initial Work' of an English lesson. This would sound ridiculous. But this is what we do in mini-lessons. This dimensions leaves mini-lessons so partial and incomplete that added motivation is necessary for the student to organise himself well during the lesson.

The following aspects help organise mini-microteaching as part of a training programme:

1. It is most advantageous to divide *the Group* of student teachers into *batches* of, say, *16 each* in which a sub-group of 8 students will give the mini-lessons in two *teams* of 4 each. In other words as much as possible a regular lesson should have four steps which each student in the team teaching one step of the regular lesson.
2. Of the 16 students 8 will give mini-lessons while the next sub-group of 8 students will function as the 'Peer Group' for the teaching. Each sub-group can similarly take turn. This adjustment is important to keep the work going smoothly.
3. The work requires *two consecutive* periods of 40 minutes each which when combined should leave enough room for a short *feedback session*. It should be possible in a ideal situation to have a short feedback session after one team (4) finishes one regular lesson and another session after the next 4 finish the round.
4. At a given time depending on the size of the Group of students such batches of 16 each can give on the lessons in a simultaneous manner or the lesson can be worked out in consecutive sessions.
5. Again, as far as the need for a cycle of (a) teach sessions, (b) feedback sessions and (c) re-teach sessions each institution may organise the sequence the way feasible to it. We may ordinarily envisage these three sessions for a sub-group of 8 students or for a team of 4 students. These details should be worked out by the particular institution.
6. The guidance cum evaluation of a mini-lesson can be done either by means of a regular tally system based on a set of evaluation points for every lesson or by means of short but upto the point comments the supervisor can record on the journal.

Mini-micro-teaching is an effective teacher training method as an initiation into the practices of the regular classroom. This method loses all its value and validity if the students lose sight of the fact that what he is doing in the mini-lesson is just a component of the regular classroom. This recurring and constant vision of the actual classroom and of the actual teaching work alone can justify mini-microteaching and its stand as a teacher education method. It is certainly a systemic approach to the training in component abilities, provided a holistic view of teaching is retained. It is a scientific way of training student teachers in the component abilities of the various aspects of classroom teaching. The ultimate focus should always be the development of these component abilities or the skills of teaching.

Bibliography

Agard, Frederik B. and Harold B. Dunkal. 1948, *An Investigation of Second Language Teaching*, Boston: Ginn and Company

Allen, J.P.B. and S. Pit Corder. 1975, *The Edinburgh Course in Allied Linguistics*, London: Oxform University Press.

Allen, D.W. and Ryan, K.A. 1969, *Microteaching*, Addison - Wesley, London.

Allen, Harold, B. (ed.) 1964, *Readings in Applied English Linguistics*, New York: Appleton—Century—Crofts.

------------------1965, *Teaching English as a Second Language: A Book of Readings*: New York : McGraw-Hill.

Allport, G.W. 1961, *Pattern and Growth in Personality*, New York : Holt, Rinehart & Winston.

Anderson, J., B.H. Durton, and C. Katz. 1969, *Study Methods A Practical Guide*, Australia: McGraw-Hill.

Anderson, Theodore. 1953, *The Teaching of Foreign Languages in Elementary School*, Boston, D.C. Health and Company.

Andrews, R. 1971, *Mocroteaching Methods: A Critique*, University of London, Institte of Education Bulletin, 23; 21-30.

Axelrod, Saul. 1977, *Behaviour Modification for the Classroom Teacher*, New York: McGraw-Hill.

Ausbel, D.P. 1963, *The Psychology of Meaningful Verbal learning*, New York: Gruce and Stratton.

Bansal, R.K. & J.B. Harrison. 1972, *Spoken English for India: A Manual of Speech and Phonetics*, Madras: Orient Longman.

------------1966, The Intelligibility of Indian English, Ph.D. Thesis, University of London.

Baruah, T.C. 1984, *The English Teacher's Handbook*, New Delhi: Sterling Publishers Pvt. Ltd.

Berlyne. D.E. 1962, *Conflict, Arousal and Curiosity*, New York: McGraw-Hill.

Berko, Jean 1958, *The Child's Learning of English Morphology*, Word, 14: 150-77, In Sapporta, Psycholinguistics, New York: Holt, Rinehart & Winston (1961),

Bishop, A.J. and Whitfield, R.C. 1972, *Situations in Teaching*, McGraw-Hill.

Bloch, Bernard, and G.L. Trager 1952, *Outline of Lingustic Analysis*, Texas: Linguistic Society of America.

Bloom, B.S. 1971, *Handbook of Summative and Evaluative Learning*, McGraw-Hill Publishing Company.

Bloomfield, Leonard, 1933, *Language*, New York: Hold, Rinerhart & Winston.

Boas, Franz, 1940, *Language and Culture*, New York : Macmillan.

Brooks, Nelson, 1964, *Language and Language Learning—Theory and Practice*, New York: Harcourt, Brace & Co.

Brown, George, 1975, *Microteaching : A Programme of Teaching Skills*, London: Metheun and Co.

Brown, Roger, and U. Bellugi, 1964, *Three Processes in the Child's Acquisition of Syntax*, Harward Educational Review, 34: 133-51.

Brumfit, C.J. 1983, *A Short Introduction to Language and Language Teaching*, Batsford Academic.

Bucky, M. 1968, The Role of games in language teaching, *Audio-visual Language Journal* (London), 5,3 125-8.

Burton, S.H. 1983, *Matering English Language*, Macmillan.

Cardenas, D. 1961, *Applied Linguistics : Spanish. A Guide for Teachers*, Boston: D.C. Health & Co.

Carrol, Jogn, B. 1953, *The Study of Language*, Cambridge, Massechusetts: Harward University Press.

--------------1959, Modern Language Aptitude Test, New York: Psychological Corporation.

-------------1964, *Language and Thought* (Foundations of Modern Psychology Series), New York: Prentice-Hall.

-------------and Roy O. Freedle, 1972, *Language Comprehension and Acquisition of Knowledge*, Washington D.C.: Winston.

Cartwright & Cartwright, 1974, *Developing Observation Skills*, New York : McGraw-Hill.

Cave, George N. 1972, From controlled to free composition, *English Language Teaching* (London) 26,3: 262-9.

Chomsky, Noam, 1957, *Syntactic Structures*, The Hague: Mouton & Co.

--------------1965, *Aspects of the Theory of Syntax*, Cambridge, Mass. : M.I.T. Press.

--------------1967, *The formal nature of language in 'Biological Foundations of Language'* (see Lenneberg, 1967).

-------------1972, *Language and Mind*, New York: Harcourt, Brace, Jovanovich, Inc. First Published in 1968.

--------------and Morris Halle, 1968, *The Sound Pattern of English*, New York : Harper & Row Publishers.

Collins, M. 1965, *Students into Teachers*, Routledge & Penguin.

Cook, M. 1970, *Interpersonal Perception*, London: Penguin.

Courts, Doughlas C. 1968, *Linguistics in the College of Education,* Education for Teaching (London) 76: 65-9.

Dacany, FE. R. 1963, *Techniques and Procedures in Second Language Teaching.* edtied by J. Donals Bowen, Quezon City: Alemar-Phoenix Publishing House.

Dale, Philip S. 1972, *Language Development; Structure and Function* Hinsdale, Illinois: The Dyden Press.

Das, Bikram K. 1973, *English for a developing country: a plea for linguistic relativism in teaching*, CIEFL (Hyderabad) 9: 18-26.

-------------1975, Educational Television in the Indian Context—a language teachers' point of view, *CIEFL Bulletin* (Hyderabad) 11: 73:82.

Datta, Sunanda. 1973, The Pronunciation of English by Bengali Speakers, *CIEFL Bulletin* (Hyderabad), 9 : 35-40.

Davis, I.F. 1973, *The Management of Learning*, New York: McGraw-Hill, New Jersey: Prentice-Hall.

Deutsch, Karl. 1953, *Nationalism and Social Communication*, Cambridge, Mass. : M.I.T. Press.

Dinneen, F.P. 1967, *An Introduction to General Linguistics*, New York: Holt, Rinehart & Winston.

Dodson, C.J. 1957, *Language Teaching and the Billingual Method*, London: Sir Isaac Pitman & Sons Ltd.

Dunkel, Harold. 1948, *Second Language Learning*, Boston: Ginn & Co.

Dunkin, M. and Biddle, B. 1973, *The Study of Teaching*, New York: Holt.

Entwistle, W.J. 1957, *Aspects of Language*, London: Faber & Faber.

Evans, D.R. 1970, *Microteaching: An Innovation in Teacher Education*, Education in Eastern Africa, 1.

Evans, T. 1982, *Teaching English*, London: Croom Helm.

Fernal, Grace 1943, *Remedial Techniques in Basic School subjects*, McGraw-Hill, New York.

Elipovic, Rudolf (ed.) 1972, *Active Methods and Modern Aids in the Teaching of Foreign Language*, London: Oxford Uni. Press.

Finocchiaro, Mary. 1964, *Teaching Children Foreign Languages*, New York: Mc-Graw-Hill.

Fisherman, Joshua A. (ed.) 1968, *Readings in the Sociology of Language*, The Hague: Mouton.

Fisher and Terry, 1977, *Children's Language and the Language Arts*, New York: McGraw-Hill.

Fotitch, T. (ed.) 1961, *Teaching Foreign Languaes in the Modern World*, Washington D.C. : Catholic University of America Press.

Foster, B. 1968, *The Changing English Language*, London: Macmillan.

Francis, Nelson W. 1958, *The Structure of American English*, New York: Ronal Press Co.

Friegebaum, I. 1965, The Cultural Setting of Language teaching, English Language Teaching Forum (Washington D.C.) 3, 4:11-13.

Fries, Charles C. 1940, *American English Grammer*, Iowa: Meredith Publishing Company.

-----------1945, *Teaching and Learning English as a Foreign Language*, Michigan: University of Michigan Press.

-----------1952, *The Structure of English*, New York: Harcourt.

-----------1963: *Linguistics and Reading*, New York: Holt.

Fowler, Mary E. 1965, *Teaching Languages, Composition and Literature*, New York: McGraw-Hill.

Gale, J.A. 1974, *Group Work in Schools*, Australia: McGraw-Hill.

Gattegno, Caleb. 1972, *Teaching Foreign Languages in Schools, the Silent Way*, New York: Educational Solutions.

Gauntlet, J.O. 1957, *Teaching English as a Foreign Language*, London, Macmillan.

Gleason, H.A. Jr. 1961, *An Introduction to Descriptive Linguistics*, New York: Holt, Rinehart & Winston.

------------1965, *Linguistics and English Grammar*, New York: Holt.

George, P.T. 1973, Teaching the mechanics of reading to beginners of English—the case for a return to a traditional approach, *CIEFL Bulletin* (Hyderabad) 9: 6-17.

Grazia, Alfred De, and Sohn, David A. (eds.) 1964, *Programmes, Teachers and Machines*. New York: Bantam Books.

Greenberg, Joseph. (ed.) 1963, *Universals of Language*, Cambridge, M.I.T. Press.

Greene, Judith, 1972, *Psycholinguistics: Chomsky and Psychology*, Middlesex: Penguin Books.

Gurry, P. 1955, *Teaching English as a Foreign Language*, London: Macmillan.

------------1962, *Teaching of English Grammar*, London: Longmans.

Hall, Edward T. 1959, *The Silent Language*, New York: Doubleday & Co.

Hall, Robert A. Jr. 1960, *Linguistics and Your Language*, New York: Doubleday & Company.

------------1964, *Introductory Linguistics*, Philadelphia: Chilton.

------------1966, *New Ways to Learn a Foreign Language*, New York: Bantam Books.

Halliday, A.M.K. 1968, **Language and Experience**, *Educational Review* (Birmingham) 20. 2: 95—106.

------------1972, *Explorations in the Functions of Language*, London:

Edward Arnold.

------------Mcinthosh, A., and Strevens, P. 1964, *The Linguistics Sciences and Language Teaching*, London: Longmans.

Haring and Schiefelbusch. 1967, *Methods in Special Education*, (with introduction to educational technology), New York: McGraw-Hill.

Harley, B. (UNESCO) 1973, *A Synthesis of Teaching Methods* (2nd ed.) Australia: McGraw-Hill.

Harmer, J. 1983, *The Practice of English Language Teaching*, Longman.

Harris, David P. 1969, *Testing English as a Foreign Language*, New York; McGraw-Hill

Haris, Zellig. 1961, *Methods in Structural Linguistics*, Chicago; The University of Chicago Press.

Harold, Hungerford, 1970, *English Linguistics*, Scot, Foresman & Co.

Hill, Archibald A. 1958, *Introduction to Linguistics Structures*, New York: Harcourt, Brace and World.

Hill, L.A. 1968, *Prepositions and Adverbial Particles*, London; Oxford University Press.

Hockett, Charles F. 1968, *A Course in Modern Linguistics*, New York: Macmillan.

-----------1967, Language, *Mathematics and Linguistics*, The Hague: Mouton.

Hoenigswald, Henry M. 1960, *Language Change and Linguistic Reconstruction*, Chicago: The University of Chicago Press.

Huebener, Theodore, 1961, *Why Johnny Should Learn Foreign Languages*, New York and Philadelphia: Chilton.

Hughes, Jogn P. 1968, *Linguistics and Language Teaching*, New York: Random House.

Hymes, Dell, 1964, *Language in Culture and Society: A Reader in Linguistics and Anthropology*, New York: Harper & Row.

Hymes, Dell. H. 1966, On Comunicative Competence, In C.J. Brumfit and K. Jognson: *The Communicative Approach to Language Teaching*. Oxford, OUP.

Jacobson, R. and M. Halle, 1956, *Fundamentals of Language*, The Hague: Mouton.

Jespersen, Otto, 1904, *How to Teach a Foreign Language*, London: George Allen & Unwin Ltd.

------------1909-1924, *A Modern English Grammar* (7 volumes), London: George Allen & Unwin.

------------1922. *Language: Its Nature, Development and Origin*, London; George Allen & Unwin.

------------1958, *The Philosphy of Grammar*, London: George Allen.

Johnson, Keith, and Keith Morrow, 1981, *Communication in the Classroom*, Longman.

Jones, J. Allen, 1968, English Language Teaching in a Social/Cultural Dilect situation: 1. English Language Teaching (London) 22. 3: 199-205.

Jones, Daniel, 1940, *An outline of English Phonetics*, 6th edition, E,P. Dutton & Co. Inc. New York.

------------1968, *Everyman's English Pronuncing Dictionary*, Edited by A.C. Gimson, The English Language Book Society, Reprinted Thirteenth E.L.B.S. Edition.

Kantk, V.Y. 1976, The Future of English Studies, *CIEFL Bulletin* (Hyderabad) 12: 41-47.

Katz, J.J. 1972, *Semantic Theory*, London: Harper & Row.

------------and J.A. Fodor, 1963, *The Structure of a Semantic Theory Language* (Baltimore) 39: 170-210.

------------and P.M. Postal, 1964, *An Integrated Theory of Semantic Descriptions*, Cambridge: M.I.T. Press.

Kolers, Paul A. 1968, Bilingualism and information processing, *Scientific American*, 218: 78-86.

Kounin, J. 1970, *Discipline and Group Management in Classroms*, New York: Holt, Rinehart & Winston.

Lado, robert, 1964, *Language Teaching: A Scientific Approach*, New York: McGraw-Hill.

------------1964, *Language Testing: The Construction and Use of Foreign Language Tests*, New York: McGraw-Hill.

------------1957, *Linguistics Across Cultures*, Ann Arbor: The University of Michigan Press.

Lamberts, J.J. 1972, *A Short Introduction to English Usage*, New York: McGraw-Hill.

Langacker, Ronald W. 1972, *Fundamentals of Linguistics Analysis*, New York: Harcourt, Brace, Jovanovich, Inc.

Lee, W.R. 1969, Some Points about aims and means in the foreign languae course, *English Language Teaching* (London) 23. 2: 100-107.

Lee, A, Jacobus, 1978, *Improving College Reading*, New York: Harcourt.

Leech, Geoffrey N. 1968, *A Linguistics Guide to English Poetry*, London: Longmans.

Leech & Svartvick, 1973, *A Communicative Grammar of English*, Longmans.

Lenneberg, E.H. 1967, *Biological Foundations of Language*, New York: John Wiley & Sons. Inc.

Lewis, M.M. 1963, *Language, Thought and Personality*, New York: Basic Books, Inc.

Lett, W.R. 1974, *The Creative Artist at Work*, Australia: McGraw-Hill.

Littlewood, W. 1983, *Communicative Language Teaching: An Introduction*, Cambridge University Press.

Logan and Logan. 1971, *A Design for Creative Teaching*, Canada, McGraw-Hill Ryereson Ltd.

Lumsdaine, A.A., and Robert Glaser, 1960, *Teaching Machines and Programmed Learning*, Washington D.C.: National Educational Association.

Lunt, Helen (Ed.) 1972, *Language and Language Teaching: Current Research in Britain*, 1871-1972, London: Longman.

Luria, A.R. 1965, *Higher Cortical Functions in Man*, New York: Basic Books, Inc.

Lyons, Jogn. 1968, *Introduction ofTheoretical Linguistics*, Cambridge University Press.

Mackey, William Francis, 1965, *Language Teaching Analysis*, London: Longmans.

------------1968, The New Technology of Teacher Training, *English Language Teaching* (London) 23. 1: 10-14.

Maley A. 1982, *Drama Techniques in Language Learning*, 2nd ed, Cambridge University Press.

Macnamara, John, 1966, *Bilngualism and Primary Education: A Survery of Irish Experience*, Edinburgh: University Press.

Mcluhan, Marshall, 1962, *Understanding Media*, Routledge & Kegan Paul.

Marty, Fernand, 1960, *Language Laboratory Learning*, Wellesley, Mass, Audio-Visual Publications.

Masayuki, Swashima, and Franklin S. Cooper, 1977, *Dynamic Aspects of Speech Production*, Tokyo.

Mathews, P.H. 1974, *Morphology : An Introduction to the Theory of Word Structure*, London: Cambridge University Press.

Mathieu, G. (ed.) 1966, *Advances in the Teaching of Modern Language*, Vol. 2. London: Pergamon Press.

McCrimmon, James M, 1976, *The Psychology of Human Learning: An Introduction*, Revised by A.L. Irion, New York:

Longmans, Green and Co.

Menyuk, P. 1969, *Sentences Children Use, Cambridge*: M.I.T. Press.

Michael, Joseph (ed.) 1967, *Foreign Language Teaching*, New York: Macmillan.

Miller, George A. 1951, *Language and Communication*, New York : McGraw-Hill.

Morris, C.W. 1955. Signs, Language, and Behaviour. New York: Prentice-Hall.

Morris, Jogn, 1972, *Creative Reading, English Language Teaching*, (London) 26. 3 : 257–61.

------------ (1972), Intensive Reading, *English Language Teaching*, (London) 27. 1 : 38–47.

Mouton, William G. 1966, *A Linguistics Guide to Language Learning*, New York: Modern Language Associations of America.

Mukalel J. & Shabbir Ahmed, 1984, *Teaching English in India*, Delhi: Arya Book Depot.

Nagarajan S. 1976, University departments of English formation of a literary public in India, *CIEFL Bulletin* (Hyderabad) 12: 49-54.

Newmark, Maxim. (ed.) 1948, *Twentieth Century Modern Language: Sources and Readings*, New York: Philosophical Library.

Nichols, R.G. 1957, *Are You Listening*, New York: McGraw-Hill.

Nida, Eugena A. 1957, *Learning a Foreign Language*, Michigan: Friendship Press.

------------1964, *Toward a Science of Translating*, Leiden: E.J. Brill.

Nikson, Marilyn, 1971, *Educational Technology*, London.

North-east Conference, 1961, Seymour L. Flaxman, (Ed.), *Modern Language Teaching in School and College*,

-----------1962. William F. Bottiglia (ed.) *Current Issues in Language Teaching.*

-----------1964, George Frewick Jones (ed.) *Foreign Language Teaching Ideals and Practices.*

-----------1965, G. Reginals Bishom (ed.), *Foreign Language Teaching: Challenges to the Profession.*

-----------1967, Thomas E. Bird (ed.), *Foreign Languages: Reading, Literature and Requirements.*

Ogden, C.K. and Richards, I.A. 1923, *The Meaning of Meaning*, New York: Harcourt, Brace & World.

Osgod, Charles, E., and Thomas A. Sebeok, 1954, Psycholinguistics: *A Survey of Theory and Research Problems*, Baltimore: Waverly Press.

Palmer, Harold, Ed. 1964, *The Principles of Language Study*, London: Oxford University Press, First Published in 1921, by Harra P. London.

-----------1921, *The Oral Way of Teaching Language*, Cambridge: W. Heffer and Sons.

-----------and V. Redman. 1968, *The Language Learning Business*, London: Oxford University Press.

Pande, M.P. 1976, Some Reflections on the use of Literature on Language Teaching, *CIEFL Bulletin* (Hyderabad) 12: 55-59.

Parry, Sylvia, 1968, Teaching Handwriting, *English Language Teaching* (London) 22.8: 235-42.

Patnaik, B.N. 1976, Contrastive Analysis and its Pedagogic Implicatios, *CIEFL Bulletin* (Hyderabad) 12: 15-27.

Paulston, Christina B. 1974, Linguistic and Communicative Competence, *TESOL Quarterly*. 8.4.

Pearson. Antony, 1968, Reflections on the use of simplified texts,

English Language Teaching (London) 22.3 242-6.

Perren, George, 1972, New Language and Yonger Children, *English Language Teaching*, (London) 26.3: 229-33.

Pike, Kenneth, 1946, *The Intonation of American English*, Michigan: The University of Michigan Press.

Pincas, Anita, 1968, 'Transformational', 'Generative' and the EFL teacher, *English Language Teaching* (London) 22.3: 210-20.

Politzer, Robert L, 1965, *Foreign Language Learning: A Linguistic Introduction*, New Jersey: Prentice-Hall.

Postal, P.M. 1968, *Aspects of Phonological Theory*, New York: Harper & Row.

Prator, C.H. Jr. 1957, *A Manual of American English Pronunciation*, Re-ed, New York: Holt, Rinehart & Winston.

Pride, J.B. and Jenet Holmes, (eds.) 1972, *Sociolinguistics*, Middlesex: Penguine Books.

Randall, Geoff. 1972, *Teaching Strategies in Primary School English*, Australia, McGraw-Hill,

Richey, Tobert W, 1973, *Planning Teaching*, (5th edition) Introduction to Education, New York: McGraw-Hill,

Rivers, Wilga M, 1964, *The Psychologist and The Foreign Language Teacher*, Chicago: University of Chicago Press,

------------1968, *Teaching Foreign Language Skills*, Chicago: University of Chicago Press,

Rivers, Wilga M, 1983, *Communicating Naturally in a Second Langauge*, Cambridge University Press,

Roberts, Reg, 1972, Aims and Objectives in Language Teaching, *English Language Teaching* (London) 26,3: 224-9,

Robey, Cora L,, Alice M, Hendrik, and Ethelyn H, Morgan, 1978, *Handbook of Basic Writing Skills*, New York: Harcourt

Robins, R,H, 1064, *General Linguistics: An Introductory Survey*, London: Longmans,

Robinsons, W,R, 1972, *Language and Social Behaviour*, Middlesex, Penguin Books,

Sadanand, Kamlesh, 1975, An Experimental Course in Spoken English, *CIEFL Bulletin* (Hyderabad) 11: 39-55,

Saporta, Sol (ed,) 1961, *Psycholinguistics: A Book of Readings*, New York: Hold, Rinehart & Winston,

Sastri, M,I, 1973, Language and Effect in Poetry, *CIEFL Bulletin* (Hyderabad) 9: 1-18,

Saussure, Ferdinand De, 1974, *Course in General Linguistics*, trans, by Peter Owen (London),

Savinquon, Sandra J, 1984, *Communicative Competence Theory & Classroom Practice*, Massa, (U,S,A,); Addison-Wesley,

Scherer, George A,C, and Michael Wertheimer, 1964, *A Pshcylinguistic Experiment in Foreign Language Teaching*, New York: McGraw-Hill,

Seaton, B, 1982, *A Handbook of English Language Teaching Terms and Practice*, Macmillan,

Shah, P,P, 1982, *English for Knowledge*, Lucknow: Print House (India),

Shipley, C,M, 1972, *A Synthesis of Teaching Methods* (3rd edition) Canada: McGraw-Hill Ryerson Ltd.

Singh, Amrik, 1968, Bilingual Method of Teaching English found simple. University News (New Delhi) 6, 5 : 14 and 17.

Skinner, B.F. 1957, Verbal Behaviour, New York : Appleton-Century-Crofts.

Smethurst, Wood Dr. 1975. Teaching Children to Read. New York: McGraw-Hill.

Smith, B,O, 1971, *Research in Teacher Education*, New York: Prentice-Hall,

Smith G,P, 1975, Some difficulties of Telugu Students, *CIEFL Bulletin* (Hyderabad): 57-72,

Smith, Henry Lee, 1956, *Linguistic Science and the Teaching of English*, Massachusetts: Haward University Press,

Stack, Edward M, 1966, *The Language Laboratory and Modern Language Teaching* : New York: Oxford University Press,

Stevick, E,W, 1963, *A workbook in Language Teaching with Special Reference to English as a Foreign Language*, New York: Abingdon Press.

Strevens, P.D. 1965, *Papers in Language and Language Teaching*, London; Oxford Univesity Press.

Thundy, Zacharia, 1976, The Origins of Indian English, *CIEFL Bulletin* (Hyderabad) 12: 29-40.

Titone, Renze, 1968, *Teaching Foreign Languages: An Historical Sketch*, Washington D.C. George Town University Press.

Turner, John D. (ed.) 1968, *Programming for the Language Laboratory*, London: University of London Press.

Valdman, Albert, 1966, *Trends in language Teaching*, New York: McGraw-Hill.

Valette, Rebecca, M. 1964, Some Reflections of Second Language, Learning, *Language Learning* (Michigan) 14: 91-98.

------------1967, *Modern Language Testing*: A Handbook, New York: Harcourt, Brace & World.

Velayudhan, S. 1978, A Workbook in English Phonetics and Phonetic Transcription, Tellicherry Printers, Kerala.

------------1978, *Contrastive Sound Structures of English and Malayalam*, Tellichery Printers, Kerala.

------------1977, *An Introduction to the Phonetics and Structure of English*, Somaiya Publications, Bombay.

Wardhaugh, Ronald, 1972, *Introduction to Linguistics*, New York: McGraw-Hill.

Weiss, A.P. 1925, Linguistics and Psychology, *Language* 1: 52-57.

Werner, H. and Bernard Kaplan 1964, *Symbol Formation*, New York: John Wiley and Sons.

West, Michael, 1941, *Learning to Read a Foreign Language*, London; Longmans.

------------1953, A General Service List of English Words, London: Longmans.

Whitehall, Harold, 1956, *Structural Essential of English*, New York: Harcourt, Brace & World.

Whorf, benjamin, 1956, *Language, Thought and Reality*, Cambrdge: M.I.T. Press.

Wilkins, D.A. 1972, *Linguistics in Language Teaching*, London: Edward Arnold.

Windsor, Lewis, J. 1973, *A Concise Pronuncing Dictionary of British and American English*, London: Oxford University Press.

Wise, Claude, M. 1955, *Applied Phonetics*, New Jersey: Prentice-Hall.

Wittich and Schuller: *Audio-Visual Materials*, Harper & Brothers, New York.

Woolf & Woolf, 1957, *Remedial Reading*, New York: McGraw-Hill.

Wragg,. E.G. 1975, *Teaching Teaching*, London : David & Charles.

Index